THE VIETNAM WAR

History SparkNotes

Spark Educational Publishing
A Division of Barnes & Noble Publishing
120 Fifth Avenue
New York, NY 10011
www.sparknotes.com

ISBN 1-4114-0426-2

Please submit all comments and questions or report errors to *www.sparknotes.com/errors*.

Printed and bound in the United States

CONTENTS

OVERVIEW

The Vietnam War is likely the most problematic of all the wars in American history. It was a morally ambiguous conflict from the start, ostensibly a war against Communism yet also a war to suppress nationalist self-determination. The war was rife with paradoxes: in the name of protecting democracy, the United States propped up a dictatorial regime in South Vietnam; later in the war, the U.S. military was destroying villages in order to "save" them. Because U.S. objectives were often poorly defined during the course of the war, U.S. policy often meandered: indeed, the United States would "Americanize" the war only to "Vietnamize" it five years later. Not surprisingly, a profound sense of confusion pervaded the entire conflict: the American media sometimes represented tactical victories as terrible defeats, while the U.S. military kept meticulous enemy body counts without any clear method of distinguishing the bodies of the hostile Viet Cong from those of the friendly South Vietnamese.

The U.S. involvement in Vietnam is inseparable from the larger context of the Cold War. Ever since the end of World War II, the United States and Soviet Union had been in the midst of a worldwide struggle for spheres of influence, each superpower wanting to exert cultural, political, and ideological control over various regions of the globe. At the same time, the United States and the USSR each wanted to stop the other country from gaining any such spheres. Southeast Asia in general, and Vietnam in particular, were important spheres of influence in the minds of both U.S. and Soviet leaders. With the "fall" of North Vietnam to Communism in 1954, the United States became committed to stopping the further spread of Communism in the region.

The escalation period of the Vietnam War, from 1955 to 1965, mirrored the Cold War in that the United States and USSR avoided direct conflict—and thereby the possibility of nuclear war—by operating through proxy governments and forces. Unfortunately for the United States, the U.S.-backed South Vietnamese government was weak and corrupt, while the Soviet-backed North Vietnamese government was a fiercely proud and independent group of nationalists willing to fight endlessly against foreign dominance and for Vietnamese unification.

The United States further antagonized the North Vietnamese by stepping into the power void that France, the former colonial power in Vietnam, had left behind. In its zeal to battle Communism, the United States essentially ended up assuming the hated role of imperial master in Vietnam. As a result, when the United States sent troops into the territory in the mid-1960s, they found a far different situation than any other they had faced up to that point in the Cold War. Instead of its usual tentative dance of brinksmanship with the USSR, the United States suddenly faced an enemy that believed deeply in its nationalist as well as Communist cause and implacably hated U.S. intervention.

Although Lyndon Johnson originally believed that the commitment of U.S. troops would save South Vietnam from Communist oppression, his policy of escalation, combined with Richard Nixon's later bombing campaigns, effectively destroyed the country. By the end of the war, the U.S. military had used 7 million tons of bombs on Vietnam—more than all the bombs dropped on Europe and Japan during World War II. The ultimate human cost of the Vietnam War was staggering for all sides: an estimated 2 million Vietnamese civilians, 1.1 million North Vietnamese soldiers, 200,000 South Vietnamese soldiers, and 58,000 U.S. soldiers were killed.

The Vietnam War had a tremendous impact on American society and culture, in large part because it was the first American war to be televised. As a result, the American press played a significant, unforeseen role in the war, especially in the arena of public opinion. The photographs, videos, and opinions of American journalists, coupled with the simple fact that young Americans were dying on foreign soil against an enemy that did not threaten the United States directly, turned much of the American public against the war. This enormous power of the media and public distrust of the government have been a mainstay of American society ever since. Decades later, the war still figures prominently in American film and literature, and the black granite wall of the Vietnam Veterans Memorial in Washington, D.C., remains one of the most potent symbols of American loss.

Summary of Events

Imperialism and Colonialism

The Vietnam War has roots in **Vietnam**'s centuries of domination by imperial and colonial powers—first **China**, which ruled ancient Vietnam, and then **France**, which took control of Vietnam in the late 1800s and established **French Indochina**. In the early 1900s, nationalist movements emerged in Vietnam, demanding more self-governance and less French influence. The most prominent of these was led by Communist leader **Ho Chi Minh**, who founded a militant nationalist organization called the **Viet Minh**.

The First Indochina War

During **World War II**, when France was occupied by Nazi Germany, it lost its foothold in Vietnam, and **Japan** took control of the country. The Viet Minh resisted these Japanese oppressors and extended its power base throughout Vietnam. When Japan surrendered at the end of World War II in 1945, Ho Chi Minh's forces took the capital of **Hanoi** and declared Vietnam to be an independent country, the **Democratic Republic of Vietnam**.

France refused to recognize Ho's declaration and returned to Vietnam, driving Ho's Communist forces into northern Vietnam. Ho appealed for aid from the **United States**, but because the United States was embroiled in the escalating **Cold War** with the Communist **USSR**, it distrusted Ho's Communist leanings and aided the French instead. Fighting between Ho's forces and the French continued in this **First Indochina War** until 1954, when a humiliating defeat at **Dien Bien Phu** prompted France to seek a peace settlement.

Divided Vietnam

The **Geneva Accords** of 1954 declared a cease-fire and divided Vietnam officially into **North Vietnam** (under Ho and his Communist forces) and **South Vietnam** (under a French-backed emperor). The dividing line was set at the **17th parallel** and was surrounded by a demilitarized zone, or **DMZ**. The Geneva Accords stipulated that the divide was temporary and that Vietnam was to be reunified under free elections to be held in 1956.

4 🍁 HISTORY SPARKNOTES

THE COLD WAR AND THE DOMINO THEORY

At this point, the United States' Cold War foreign policy began to play a major part in Vietnam. U.S. policy at the time was dominated by the **domino theory**, which believed that the "fall" of North Vietnam to Communism might trigger all of Southeast Asia to fall, setting off a sort of Communist chain reaction. Within a year of the Geneva Accords, the United States therefore began to offer support to the anti-Communist politician **Ngo Dinh Diem**. With U.S. assistance, Diem took control of the South Vietnamese government in 1955, declared the **Republic of Vietnam**, and promptly canceled the elections that had been scheduled for 1956.

THE DIEM REGIME

Diem's regime proved corrupt, oppressive, and extremely unpopular. Nonetheless, the United States continued to prop it up, fearful of the increasing Communist resistance activity it noted in South Vietnam. This resistance against Diem's regime was organized by the Ho Chi Minh–backed **National Liberation Front**, which became more commonly known as the **Viet Cong**.

In 1962, U.S. president **John F. Kennedy** sent American "military advisors" to Vietnam to help train the South Vietnamese army, the **ARVN**, but quickly realized that the Diem regime was unsalvageable. Therefore, in 1963, the United States backed a coup that overthrew Diem and installed a new leader. The new U.S.-backed leaders proved just as corrupt and ineffective.

JOHNSON AND U.S. ESCALATION

Kennedy's successor, **Lyndon B. Johnson**, pledged to honor Kennedy's commitments but hoped to keep U.S. involvement in Vietnam to a minimum. After North Vietnamese forces allegedly attacked U.S. Navy ships in the **Gulf of Tonkin** in 1964, however, Johnson was given carte blanche in the form of the **Gulf of Tonkin Resolution** and began to send U.S. troops to Vietnam. Bombing campaigns such as 1965's **Operation Rolling Thunder** ensued, and the conflict escalated. Johnson's **"Americanization"** of the war led to a presence of nearly 400,000 U.S. troops in Vietnam by the end of 1966.

QUAGMIRE AND ATTRITION

As the United States became increasingly mired in Vietnam, it pursued a strategy of **attrition**, attempting to bury the Vietnamese Communist forces under an avalanche of casualties. However, the Viet Cong's **guerrilla tactics** frustrated and demoralized U.S. troops,

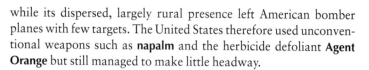

while its dispersed, largely rural presence left American bomber planes with few targets. The United States therefore used unconventional weapons such as **napalm** and the herbicide defoliant **Agent Orange** but still managed to make little headway.

The Tet Offensive

In 1968, the North Vietnamese Army and the Viet Cong launched a massive campaign called the **Tet Offensive**, attacking nearly thirty U.S. targets and dozens of other cities in South Vietnam at once. Although the United States pushed back the offensive and won a tactical victory, American media coverage characterized the conflict as a defeat, and U.S. public support for the war plummeted. Morale among U.S. troops also hit an all-time low, manifesting itself tragically in the 1968 **My Lai Massacre**, in which frustrated U.S. soldiers killed hundreds of unarmed Vietnamese civilians in a small village.

The Antiwar Movement

Meanwhile, the **antiwar movement** within the United States gained momentum as **student protesters**, countercultural **hippies**, and even many mainstream Americans denounced the war. Protests against the war and the military **draft** grew increasingly violent, resulting in police brutality outside the **Democratic National Convention** in 1968 and the deaths of four students at **Kent State University** in 1970 when Ohio National Guardsmen fired on a crowd. Despite the protests, Johnson's successor, President **Richard M. Nixon**, declared that a **"silent majority"** of Americans still supported the war.

Vietnamization and U.S. Withdrawal

Nonetheless, Nixon promoted a policy of **Vietnamization** of the war, promising to withdraw U.S. troops gradually and hand over management of the war effort to the South Vietnamese. Although Nixon made good on his promise, he also illegally expanded the geographic scope of the war by authorizing the bombing of Viet Cong sites in the neutral nations of **Cambodia** and **Laos**, all without the knowledge or consent of the U.S. Congress. The revelation of these illegal actions, along with the publication of the secret **Pentagon Papers** in U.S. newspapers in 1971, caused an enormous scandal in the United States and forced Nixon to push for a peace settlement.

The Cease-fire and the Fall of Saigon

After secret negotiations between U.S. emissary **Henry A. Kissinger** and North Vietnamese representative **Le Duc Tho** in 1972, Nixon engaged in diplomatic maneuvering with China and the USSR—and stepped up bombing of North Vietnam—to pressure the North Vietnamese into a settlement. This **cease-fire** was finally signed in January 1973, and the last U.S. military personnel left Vietnam in March 1973.

The U.S. government continued to fund the South Vietnamese army, but this funding quickly dwindled. Meanwhile, as President Nixon became embroiled in the **Watergate scandal** that led to his resignation in August 1974, North Vietnamese forces stepped up their attacks on the South and finally launched an all-out offensive in the spring of 1975. On April 30, 1975, the South Vietnamese capital of **Saigon** fell to the North Vietnamese, who reunited the country under Communist rule as the **Socialist Republic of Vietnam**, ending the Vietnam War.

KEY PEOPLE & TERMS

PEOPLE

BAO DAI
The last emperor of Vietnam, who ascended the throne in 1926. Bao Dai proved to be an ineffective ruler and was unable to exercise any of his powers without the support of the French colonial regime. He abdicated in 1946, after the **Viet Minh** drove out the Japanese occupation forces and took control of the government. In 1949, the French reinstalled Bao Dai as the premier of "independent Vietnam" but left affairs of state to his pro-French appointees. Only one year after the **Geneva Conference** created a republic in South Vietnam, **Ngo Dinh Diem** outmaneuvered Bao Dai and took power; Bao Dai then retired to France.

MCGEORGE BUNDY
The special assistant for national security affairs under both **John F. Kennedy** and **Lyndon B. Johnson**. Bundy pressed for escalating the Vietnam War but after leaving his position in 1966 became critical of further escalation.

WILLIAM CALLEY
A U.S. Army lieutenant and the leader of the company of U.S. soldiers who killed several hundred unarmed Vietnamese civilians in the 1968 **My Lai Massacre**. A 1971 court-martial sentenced Calley to a life prison term, but many Americans believed that he was a scapegoat for larger government atrocities, and he was paroled in 1974.

DWIGHT D. EISENHOWER
The 34th U.S. president, who popularized the **domino theory** that was later used to justify increased U.S. political and military involvement in Vietnam.

J. WILLIAM FULBRIGHT
A U.S. senator from Arkansas and a leading critic of the Vietnam War in the U.S. Congress. In 1966, Fulbright published the influential book *The Arrogance of Power*, which attacked President **Lyndon B. Johnson** and the U.S. war strategy. That year, Fulbright also

chaired nationally televised hearings of the Senate Foreign Relations Committee that criticized the war.

Ho Chi Minh

The primary Vietnamese nationalist and Communist leader during the twentieth century, who resisted French, Japanese, and American influence in Vietnam. Born in poverty in French-occupied Annam, Ho traveled widely and spent considerable time in Paris, London, and New York, gaining exposure to Western ideas, including **Communism**. On his return to Vietnam, he founded the **Indochina Communist Party** in 1930 and the **Viet Minh** in 1941. From its founding to his death in 1969, Ho was president of the **Democratic Republic of Vietnam**, serving as the primary North Vietnamese leader throughout much of the Vietnam War.

Lyndon B. Johnson

The 36th U.S. president, who promised to honor his predecessor **John F. Kennedy**'s limited U.S. commitments in Vietnam but ended up escalating the war drastically after the U.S. Congress passed the **Gulf of Tonkin Resolution** in 1964. Empowered by the resolution, Johnson authorized **Operation Rolling Thunder** in 1965 to bomb North Vietnam into submission. When this failed, he sent more than 500,000 U.S. troops to Vietnam and ultimately converted the conflict into a protracted and bitter war.

George F. Kennan

A U.S. State Department analyst who first articulated the doctrine of containment in 1947, arguing that the United States could keep Communism from spreading simply by deterring Soviet expansion at critical points, mostly in Europe. The idea of containment became very influential and served as the basis of U.S. foreign policy for much of the Cold War.

John F. Kennedy

The 35th U.S. president, whose decision to send U.S. "military advisors" into Vietnam in 1962 marked the first official U.S. involvement in the country. Although Kennedy and his administration backed the corrupt **Ngo Dinh Diem** regime in South Vietnam, they ultimately decided to back a coup to overthrow Diem in November 1963. Just weeks later, Kennedy was assassinated, and Vice President **Lyndon B. Johnson** became president.

HENRY A. KISSINGER

A former political science professor who served as President **Richard Nixon**'s national security advisor and then as his secretary of state. The German-born Kissinger worked closely with Nixon to create and implement the policy of **Vietnamization** and personally engaged in negotiations with North Vietnamese emissary **Le Duc Tho** in 1972 to hammer out a **cease-fire**. Kissinger also assisted Nixon in using **China** and the **Soviet Union** to pressure North Vietnam to opt for a peace settlement.

EDWARD LANSDALE

A CIA operative based in Saigon beginning in 1953 who initiated some mostly failed psychological operations against Vietnamese Communists and spoke favorably about **Ngo Dinh Diem** to U.S. policy makers.

LE DUAN

The primary leader of the North Vietnamese Communist Party after **Ho Chi Minh**'s death in 1969.

LE DUC THO

A senior North Vietnamese diplomat who engaged in secret negotiations in Paris with U.S. emissary **Henry A. Kissinger** in 1972, leading to the **cease-fire** that ended official U.S. involvement in Vietnam in January 1973.

ROBERT S. MCNAMARA

The secretary of defense under **John F. Kennedy** and **Lyndon B. Johnson**, from 1961 to 1968. McNamara initially advocated increasing U.S. involvement in Vietnam but started to question U.S. policy by 1966. After growing disillusioned with the direction of the war, McNamara resigned his position following the **Tet Offensive** in early 1968.

NGO DINH DIEM

The U.S.-backed leader of the South Vietnamese **Republic of Vietnam** from 1955 until 1963. Diem came from a family that was both Confucian and Catholic, and though his Christianity endeared him to many U.S. policy makers, it alienated him from South Vietnam's Buddhist majority. Diem's regime quickly became corrupt and autocratic, cracking down viciously on Buddhist leaders and ignoring the **Geneva Conference**'s promise of free elections in 1956. Increasingly paranoid, he gave his family members important positions of leadership in the government, which they abused. Although the

KEY PEOPLE & TERMS

United States continued to support Diem, this support ultimately waned, and Diem and his brother **Ngo Dinh Nhu** were assassinated in 1963 as part of a U.S.-approved coup.

NGO DINH NHU

A brother of **Ngo Dinh Diem** who effectively became a warlord after Diem appointed him head of the **Can Lao**, the South Vietnamese secret police. Brutal, exploitative, and corrupt, Nhu earned the universal hatred of the South Vietnamese population. His sharp-tongued wife, **Madame Nhu**, who served as South Vietnam's de facto first lady, was equally hated. Nhu's excesses were largely responsible for the U.S.-backed coup of November 1963 in which both Diem and Nhu were assassinated.

MADAME NHU

The wife of **Ngo Dinh Nhu** and de facto first lady of the corrupt South Vietnamese government under **Ngo Dinh Diem**. Madame Nhu was a hated figure and public relations disaster, a sort of Vietnamese Marie-Antoinette who cared nothing for the struggles of Vietnamese peasants and displayed an extravagant fondness for all things French, despite the fact that the French were the hated former colonial masters of Vietnam. After a Buddhist monk publicly burned himself to death in 1963 in protest of the Diem regime, Madame Nhu derided the incident as a "barbecuing" and stated that she would provide gasoline and matches for the next monk who wanted to follow suit. She was abroad when a U.S.-backed coup toppled Diem and her husband in November 1963 and stayed away from Vietnam thereafter.

RICHARD M. NIXON

The 37th U.S. president, who orchestrated the U.S. withdrawal from Vietnam in the early 1970s. First elected in 1968, Nixon claimed amid the rising din of antiwar protests that a **"silent majority"** of Americans still supported the war. Nonetheless, he engaged in a policy of **Vietnamization** to withdraw U.S. troops from Vietnam and hand over military authority to the South Vietnamese. Meanwhile, Nixon covertly expanded the scope of the war by secretly authorizing illegal military actions in **Cambodia** and **Laos**. By 1972, he and his national security advisor, **Henry A. Kissinger**, were pursuing secret negotiations with North Vietnam and engaging in diplomacy with both **China** and the **Soviet Union** in order to pressure North Vietnam into a cease-fire. Although Nixon was reelected in a landslide in 1972, his administration became dogged with scandals ranging from **Watergate** to the **Pentagon Papers** to the public revelation of the U.S. military actions in Cambodia. Despite his skilled diplomacy and success at removing U.S. troops from Vietnam, he resigned in 1974 to avoid impeachment over the scandals.

Vo Nguyen Giap

Ho Chi Minh's leading general and the primary commander of Vietnamese Communist forces from the earliest days of the **Viet Minh**. A former lawyer and history teacher, Giap proved his military brilliance at the battle of **Dien Bien Phu** in 1954, in which he defeated the French to end the **First Indochina War** and give Vietnam more leverage at the **Geneva Conference** bargaining table. Giap remained involved in the North Vietnamese military throughout the ensuing struggle with the United States.

William C. Westmoreland

A U.S. Army general who in 1964 became the commander of the **MACV**, the corps of U.S. "military advisors" in Vietnam. As the war escalated and the United States sent troops, Westmoreland continually pushed for more U.S. ground forces in Vietnam and instituted **search-and-destroy** missions, as he believed that a war of **attrition** would result in a victory for the United States. His direction gave U.S. troops definitive goals but also tended to put them in far greater danger than ever before, and his request for an additional 200,000 troops after the 1968 **Tet Offensive** shocked the American public, who had been reassured that the United States was making substantial headway in the war.

Terms

17th Parallel

The dividing line between **North Vietnam** and **South Vietnam** as established by the 1954 **Geneva Conference**. The 17th parallel was buffered by a demilitarized zone, or **DMZ**, between the two countries.

Agent Orange

A chemical herbicide and defoliant that U.S. forces sprayed extensively in order to kill vegetation in the Vietnamese jungle and expose Viet Cong hideouts. Agent Orange inflicted immense damage on Vietnam's natural environment and led to decades of unforeseen health problems among Vietnamese civilians and U.S. military forces.

KEY PEOPLE & TERMS

ANNAM

The central of the three divisions of French colonial Vietnam, between **Tonkin** to the north and **Cochin China** to the south. The major city in Annam was **Hue**.

ARMY OF THE REPUBLIC OF VIETNAM (ARVN)

The national army of South Vietnam, which U.S. "military advisors" of the **MACV** trained beginning in 1962. By 1965, after several defeats by the Viet Cong at battles such as **Ap Bac** and **Pleiku,** the ARVN was seen as ineffective.

BINH XUYEN

The Vietnamese mafia, headquartered in a Chinese-dominated Saigon suburb of Cholon. The Binh Xuyen influenced politics in southern Vietnam under the corrupt French-backed government.

CAN LAO

The South Vietnamese secret police during the **Ngo Dien Diem** regime, which was controlled by Diem's hated brother **Ngo Dinh Nhu.**

CAO DAI

An eclectic cult in South Vietnam that combined elements of Eastern religions and Western history and culture. The Cao Dai exerted considerable influence on the corrupt French-backed government in southern Vietnam in the late 1940s.

CENTRAL OFFICE OF SOUTH VIETNAM (COSVN)

The alleged central command center that controlled all **Viet Cong** operations during the Vietnam War. Although U.S. military officials insisted that the COSVN existed, it was never found, despite exhaustive, resource-draining search campaigns by U.S. forces. It is unclear whether the COSVN ever existed at all, as the Viet Cong was notorious for decentralized guerrilla operations that were difficult to pin down or disable.

CHRISTMAS BOMBING

An intensive bombing campaign against **Hanoi** that President **Richard M. Nixon** launched in late December 1972, in an attempt to force the North Vietnamese into a peace settlement. The NVA did not surrender but instead called for a **cease-fire,** which was signed in January 1973.

COCHIN CHINA

The southernmost of the three divisions of French colonial Vietnam, below **Tonkin** and **Amman** to the north. The major city in Cochin China was **Saigon**.

COINTELPRO

The FBI's counterintelligence program, which President **Lyndon B. Johnson** authorized to spy on domestic anti–Vietnam War activists toward the end of his administration. COINTELPRO agents planted false evidence and arrested hundreds of antiwar activists on bogus charges of supporting Communism. These harsh and illegal tactics turned the American public away from the federal government and widened the **credibility gap**.

CONTAINMENT

A U.S. foreign policy strategy during the Cold War, developed in 1947 by State Department analyst **George F. Kennan**. Under containment, the United States would not challenge nations already in the **Soviet Union**'s sphere of influence but also would not tolerate any further Soviet or Communist expansion. Although containment was meant to apply primarily to Europe, it evolved into the **domino theory** that formed the basis for U.S. involvement in Vietnam.

CREDIBILITY GAP

The term applied to the difference between what the U.S. military and **Lyndon B. Johnson** were telling the American public about the Vietnam War and what the American media said was actually occurring on the ground. As a result of the credibility gap, many Americans began to question the president's honesty. This "credibility gap" widened further when Johnson authorized both the **CIA** and FBI's **COINTELPRO** to spy on antiwar activists. The credibility gap made Johnson a political liability for the Democratic Party, and he declined to run for reelection in 1968.

DEMILITARIZED ZONE (DMZ)

The no-man's-land surrounding the border between **North Vietnam** and **South Vietnam** at the **17th parallel**.

DEMOCRATIC REPUBLIC OF VIETNAM (DRV)

The **Ho Chi Minh**-led Communist government of North Vietnam which was created after the 1954 **Geneva Conference** divided the country at the **17th parallel**.

DIEN BIEN PHU

A small village in the remote, mountainous northwest corner of Vietnam that was the site of a major French defeat at the hands of the **Viet Minh** in 1954. The French attempted to lure the Viet Minh into a trap at Dien Bien Phu, where a central base with an airstrip was defended by three surrounding artillery bases. Viet Minh General **Vo Nguyen Giap**, however, had Vietnamese peasants smuggle disassembled artillery pieces into the surrounding mountains, where they were then reassembled and used to bombard the French airstrip, destroying the French supply line. The decisive battle of the **First Indochina War**, Dien Bien Phu led France to seek a peace settlement and gave the Viet Minh negotiating power at the **Geneva Conference**.

DOMINO THEORY

First popularized by President **Dwight D. Eisenhower** in 1954, the idea that if one nation fell to Communism, the surrounding nations would be likely to fall to Communism as well, starting a chain reaction in which nations fell like dominoes in a line. The domino theory guided U.S. foreign policy for years and was used to justify U.S. involvement in Vietnam.

FRAGGING

A practice, which erupted sporadically late in the Vietnam War, in which demoralized U.S. servicemen killed their own superior officers in order to avoid being sent on dangerous missions. Although fragging was not widespread, numerous specific incidents were reported.

FRENCH INDOCHINA

The French colonial term for the area encompassing present-day Cambodia, Laos, and Vietnam (which was itself composed of Tonkin, Annam, and Cochin China).

GENEVA CONFERENCE

A 1954 peace conference at the end of the **First Indochina War**, prompted by the stunning French defeat at Dien Bien Phu. The conference issued the **Geneva Accords**, which divided Vietnam officially into **North Vietnam** and **South Vietnam** along the **17th parallel** as a temporary measure and promised free Vietnam-wide elections for 1956 (although these elections never occurred).

GULF OF TONKIN RESOLUTION

A 1964 resolution, passed by a near-unanimous vote in the U.S. Congress, that gave President **Lyndon B. Johnson** a free hand to escalate the war in Vietnam. The resolution was prompted by an incident in which two U.S. Navy destroyers were allegedly attacked by North Vietnamese forces in the Gulf of Tonkin. Though not an explicit war declaration, the resolution empowered Johnson to initiate **Operation Rolling Thunder** and allowed a process of escalation that would eventually see more than 500,000 U.S. soldiers committed to the war in Vietnam.

HAO HOA
An organization in southern Vietnam that combined Buddhism and nationalism and openly opposed the French colonial government. The Hao Hoa built a sizable army and in the 1950s counted over a million people as members.

MILITARY ASSISTANCE COMMAND OF VIETNAM (MACV)
A group of U.S. "military advisors" whom President **John F. Kennedy** sent to Vietnam in 1962 to train the South Vietnamese army, the **ARVN**, to fight against the **Viet Cong**. The MACV's numbers soared steadily through the 1960s as the United States became increasingly involved in Vietnam. General **William C. Westmoreland** became head of MACV in 1964.

MY LAI MASSACRE
A 1968 raid on the tiny village of **My Lai** by an American unit in South Vietnam. The soldiers, angry and frustrated at their inability to find **Viet Cong** operatives in the village, killed up to 500 unarmed Vietnamese civilians—men, women, children, and elderly—without provocation. News of the massacre surfaced in 1969, outraging Americans and turning public opinion against the U.S. military. The leader of the company, Lieutenant **William Calley**, was court-martialed in 1971 and sentenced to a life term but later paroled.

NAPALM
A flammable, sprayable, gasoline-based gel that the U.S. military used extensively as a weapon in Vietnam. Napalm inflicted devastating burns, killing and maiming many Vietnamese soldiers and civilians.

NATIONAL LIBERATION FRONT (NLF)
An organization formed in 1960 to provide structure and support to the formerly isolated cells of the southern **Viet Cong**. Eventually, the terms NLF and Viet Cong came to be used interchangeably.

NIXON DOCTRINE

A proclamation issued by President **Richard M. Nixon** in 1969 that the United States would no longer send troops to fight Communist revolutions abroad. The doctrine, issued along with his policy of **Vietnamization**, effectively reversed the policies of several post–World War II U.S. presidents.

NSC-68

A 1950 National Security Council memo that advocated an enormous increase in U.S. military spending to combat the perceived growing threat of Communism. NSC-68 contributed to the **domino theory** that was later used to justify U.S. involvement in Vietnam.

OPERATION ROLLING THUNDER

A sustained U.S. bombing effort against North Vietnam authorized by President **Lyndon B. Johnson** in 1965 and lasting until 1968. Rolling Thunder was launched in response to a **Viet Cong** raid on a U.S. military base at **Pleiku** that killed several U.S. servicemen. When the air strikes failed to end the war, Johnson increased the number of U.S. soldiers in South Vietnam from roughly 200,000 to over 500,000.

PENTAGON PAPERS

A secret U.S. government report originally commissioned by Secretary of State **Robert S. McNamara** to detail U.S. involvement in Vietnam since World War II. In 1971, the Pentagon Papers were leaked to the *New York Times* and other newspapers and caused an uproar. When the Nixon administration attempted to block their publication, the U.S. Supreme Court issued a ruling to allow their release to continue. Because the Pentagon Papers revealed that the U.S. government had lied about numerous secret operations in Vietnam, the American public grew even more distrustful of the government.

REPUBLIC OF VIETNAM (RVN)

The corrupt, U.S.-backed government of **South Vietnam**, which **Ngo Dinh Diem** proclaimed in 1955.

SEARCH AND DESTROY

A U.S. military strategy designed to send U.S. troops out into the field proactively to locate and kill **Viet Cong** forces. The policy, instituted and supported by General **William C. Westmoreland**, stood in contrast to the previous U.S. policy to protect only **"strategic enclaves,"** those areas that the South Vietnamese government still held.

THE VIETNAM WAR 🌿 17

SILENT MAJORITY

The key words in a statement by President **Richard M. Nixon** about the antiwar movement. Nixon claimed that despite the fact that antiwar protests were becoming vocal and widespread, a "silent majority" of Americans still supported the war in Vietnam. In other words, the president claimed that noisy activists constituted only a small percentage of the American public.

STUDENTS FOR A DEMOCRATIC SOCIETY (SDS)

One of the major organizations of **antiwar protesters** in the United States during the 1960s. Founded in 1959, the quasi-socialist SDS began to organize widespread protests against the U.S. military **draft** by 1965.

TET OFFENSIVE

A massive offensive launched by **Viet Cong** guerrillas on January 30, 1968, the Vietnamese new year holiday of **Tet**. The Tet Offensive comprised simultaneous attacks on dozens of U.S.-controlled sites in South Vietnam. Although the offensive resulted in a tactical victory for the United States and many Viet Cong casualties, the American public saw it as a setback, as the U.S. military and President **Lyndon B. Johnson** had led them to believe that the Viet Cong was already well on its way to defeat. The Tet Offensive caused public support for the war to plummet in the United States, especially when the U.S. military requested 200,000 soldiers in the months following the attacks.

TONKIN

The northernmost of the three divisions of French colonial Vietnam, above **Amman** and **Cochin China** to the south. The major city in Tonkin was **Hanoi**.

TWENTY-SIXTH AMENDMENT

A 1971 amendment to the U.S. Constitution that lowered the voting age from twenty-one to eighteen. The amendment was passed in response to protests that young U.S. soldiers fighting and dying in Vietnam lacked the legal right to vote for or against the politicians who were running the war. Although antiwar activists welcomed the amendment, they continued to protest.

VIET CONG (VC)

Akin to the American slang word "Commies," an originally mildly derisive term for Communist forces in South Vietnam who opposed the U.S.-backed government in Saigon. "Viet Cong" grew to lose its

KEY PEOPLE & TERMS

negative connotation and came into common use as the war progressed. By the time of U.S. involvement, the Viet Cong was a sizable guerrilla force hidden among South Vietnam's population, making its members extremely difficult to find or target. It often worked in conjunction with the professional **North Vietnamese Army (NVA)** to attack U.S. soldiers and supply lines. The United States lost the war in Vietnam in large part due to the Viet Cong's tenacity and its widespread popularity with the South Vietnamese.

Viet Minh

Vietnamese Communist resistance forces, based in northern Vietnam and led by **Ho Chi Minh**, during the **First Indochina War** with France (1945–1954).

Vietnamization

President **Richard M. Nixon**'s 1969 plan that called for withdrawing almost all of the 500,000 U.S. troops in Vietnam over the next year and handing over more responsibility to the South Vietnamese. Although Nixon did remove troops, he also planned another intensive round of bombing in North Vietnam to convince Hanoi to end the war.

War Powers Resolution

An act passed by the U.S. Congress in 1973 after the extent of President **Richard M. Nixon**'s secret bombing campaigns in neutral Cambodia was revealed. The act required the president to notify Congress upon launching any U.S. military action abroad and limited any such action to sixty to ninety days in duration if Congress did not approve it.

Watergate

A domestic scandal in the United States that began in the summer of 1972, when police arrested five men breaking into the Democratic Party headquarters at the **Watergate Hotel** in Washington, D.C. President **Richard M. Nixon** publicly denied having any prior knowledge of the incident and created a special investigative committee to look into the matter. Eventually, it was revealed that Nixon had authorized both the break-in and the cover-up that followed. As the scandal exploded, calls arose for Nixon's impeachment; Nixon ultimately resigned in 1974. Taking advantage of the confusion and distraction in the Nixon administration, North Vietnamese forces moved into South Vietnam, setting the stage for an offensive in the spring of 1975 that led to the fall of **Saigon**.

SUMMARY & ANALYSIS

HISTORICAL BACKGROUND: 900–1900

EVENTS	
939	Vietnam gains independence from China
1279	China launches new invasion of Vietnam but is driven back
1407	China reinvades Vietnam, this time successfully
1428	Vietnamese finally drive Chinese out
1620	Vietnam is divided between Trinh in north, Nguyen in south
1858	French invade Vietnam
1862	French establish protectorate of Cochin China
1887	French merge Vietnam and Cambodia to form French Indochina
1893	French add Laos to their territory of French Indochina

ANCIENT VIETNAM

For more than a thousand years, until the middle of the tenth century, the region we today call **Vietnam** lived under the rule of imperial **China**, first under the Han dynasty and then under the T'ang dynasty. Throughout this millennium of Chinese domination, the Vietnamese people nonetheless maintained a sense of cultural independence. They even managed several fierce revolts, although these rebellions were intermittent and never met with success.

Although Vietnam gained independence from China in 939, Chinese rule returned under the Ming dynasty, and Vietnam did not become truly independent until the 1400s, when the Chinese empire weakened. By the 1600s, Vietnam was divided between two powerful families. The **Trinh** controlled northern Vietnam, with a capital at **Hanoi**. The **Nguyen** controlled the south, including the fertile Mekong River delta, and maintained a capital at **Hue**.

FRENCH COLONIALISM

In 1858, as European powers were scrambling to outdo one another in imperial wealth and power, **France** invaded Vietnam. After forcing a peace treaty in 1862, the French established a colonial government for Vietnam in the form of a protectorate that the French called **Cochin China**. Bypassing the traditional capitals of Hanoi and Hue, they instead established a colonial capital at **Saigon**, in the south of Vietnam. In 1883, France added the more northerly regions of Tonkin and Annam to its imperial holdings, and in 1893 combined all their Vietnamese and Cambodian protectorates with the territory of Laos to form **French Indochina**.

A Tradition of Resistance

Because Vietnam was controlled by other nations for so much of its history, it had a long, violent tradition of fighting against imperial overlords. These conflicts often lasted for generations, but in the end Vietnamese resolve always overcame the patience and resources of conquering powers. With a long heritage of resistance, many twentieth-century Vietnamese were prepared to fight against more powerful nations, even if it took decades and exacted a high cost in human lives.

North-South Disunity

Although much is made of the divide during the Vietnam War between U.S.-backed South Vietnam and Soviet-backed North Vietnam, this north-south split actually went back centuries, to the divide between the northern Trinh family and southern Nguyen family in the 1600s. During Vietnam's periods of independence since that time, its northern and southern halves frequently faced each other in a kind of civil war. The split between the communist North and U.S.-backed South that began in the 1950s was therefore not purely a result of the United States and USSR carving out spheres of influence—it was also an echo of a cultural division that had persisted for generations.

Mixing of Cultures

Although Vietnam fought the Chinese and the French, it also received profound cultural influences from them. The centuries of Chinese rule, for instance, brought several varieties of Buddhism that the Vietnamese adopted widely. Furthermore, the influx of the French in the late 1800s brought elements of Western society, many of which Vietnamese culture had absorbed by the 1950s. Many Vietnamese elites attended Western-style schools, spoke French more comfortably than Vietnamese, and were Catholic. Many had also spent time in Europe, where they were exposed to even more Western cultural influences than were present in Vietnam.

VIETNAMESE NATIONALISM AND THE FIRST INDOCHINA WAR: 1900–1954

EVENTS

1919	France ignores Ho Chi Minh's demands at Versailles Peace Conference
1926	Bao Dai becomes last Vietnamese emperor
1930	Ho founds Indochinese Communist Party
1940	Japan occupies Vietnam
1941	Ho founds Viet Minh
1945	Viet Minh takes Hanoi in August Revolution Ho takes power, establishes Democratic Republic of Vietnam (DRV) Truman rejects DRV's request for formal recognition
1946	First Indochina War begins
1954	Viet Minh defeat French at Dien Bien Phu

KEY PEOPLE

Ho Chi Minh	Socialist and nationalist activist; founded PCI and Viet Minh; established Democratic Republic of Vietnam in 1945
Bao Dai	Last Vietnamese emperor; took power in 1926, effectively as a French vassal; continued as figurehead until the 1950s but enjoyed little popularity
Vo Nguyen Giap	Viet Minh general; used guerrilla tactics successfully against Japanese during World War II, then orchestrated defeat of French forces at Dien Bien Phu in 1954
Harry S Truman	33rd U.S. president; rejected Ho's calls for U.S. recognition of the DRV due to worries about Ho's Communist stance

EARLY NATIONALIST MOVEMENTS

In the early twentieth century, Vietnamese nationalism against the French surged. In 1919, **Ho Chi Minh**, a Vietnamese socialist activist living in France at the time, submitted eight demands to the French at the **Versailles Peace Conference** that followed the end of World War I. The list included representation in the French parliament, freedom of speech, and release of political prisoners. When France ignored these demands, several nationalist and Communist organizations sprang up in Vietnam.

The French tried to counter the nationalist movements by appealing to traditional authority, propping up the Vietnamese emperor, **Bao Dai**, who took power in 1926. Indeed, many of the new nationalist and Communist movements in Vietnam were urban-based militant insurgencies, and none met with much success. However, the movements did create several enduring organizations, including the **Vietnamese Nationalist Party (VNQDD)**, formed in 1927, and the **Indochinese Communist Party (PCI)**, founded in 1930 by Ho Chi Minh himself.

JAPANESE RULE AND THE VIET MINH

During **World War II**, when France fell to Germany, **Japan** occupied Vietnam from 1940 to 1945. Ho saw the Japanese invasion as a chance to build up a new nationalist force, one that appealed to all aspects of Vietnamese society. Therefore, in 1941, he founded the **Viet Minh** (the League for Vietnamese Independence).

Americans opposed the Japanese in World War II, so Ho was able to convince U.S. leaders to secretly supply the Viet Minh with weapons to fight their new Japanese oppressors. General **Vo Nguyen Giap** fought successfully against the Japanese after Ho convinced him to adopt guerrilla tactics. Throughout the course of World War II, the Viet Minh successfully expanded its power base in Tonkin and Annam. It helped peasants in the region during a wartime famine, which won the organization immense popularity.

THE AUGUST REVOLUTION AND DRV

In August 1945, near the end of the war and with Japan's attention completely diverted, the Viet Minh conquered Hanoi in what became known as the **August Revolution**. Emperor Bao Dai abdicated his throne in late August, and just a week later, on September 2, the Japanese signed a formal surrender to end World War II.

Upon Japan's defeat, Ho Chi Minh declared Vietnam to be independent, naming the country the **Democratic Republic of Vietnam (DRV)**. The French did not recognize Ho's declaration, however. French forces returned to Vietnam and drove the Viet Minh into the north of the country but were unable to penetrate farther.

Later in 1945, Ho wrote a number of letters to **Harry S Truman**, the U.S. president, appealing for official U.S. recognition of the DRV. However, the United States was becoming embroiled in postwar tension with the **Soviet Union**—tension that would quickly escalate into the **Cold War**. Wary of Ho's Communist leanings, the United States refused his request, denounced him, and offered to help the French. Within a year, American ships were transporting French troops into Vietnam.

NATIONALISM AND COMMUNISM

One of the things that made the Vietnam War so morally confusing for Americans was the fact that the Viet Minh were both nationalists and Communist. Americans, brought up extolling the glory of the freedom fighters of the American Revolution, generally viewed nationalism and self- determination as a good thing. In this light, Ho Chi Minh's courageous fight against French imperialism seemed heroic. However, as the United States was a capitalist country that at the time was engaged in a paranoid ideological battle with the Communist USSR, Americans also were concerned with and frightened by Ho's socialist beliefs.

IMPORTANCE OF THE VIET MINH
Although a number of Vietnamese groups engaged in several separate nationalist initiatives against the French, only the Viet Minh finally hit on the right formula. The Viet Minh leadership was remarkably experienced, its abilities honed by a lifetime of conflicts opposing France and then reinforced by the struggle against the Japanese in World War II. The fight against Japan also helped the Viet Minh become enormously popular among the Vietnamese people.

The brilliant tactician Ho Chi Minh perfectly surveyed the political situation during World War II, playing upon the United States' anti-Japanese priorities in order to obtain weapons and supplies that would help the Viet Minh establish a northern power base. Thus, the early successes of the Viet Minh were ironically accomplished via U.S. support.

THE VIET MINH LEADERSHIP
The Viet Minh had a slew of other unusually talented and committed leaders in addition to Ho. The hawkish **Le Duan** controlled DRV guerrilla operations in southern Vietnam. **Truong Chinh**, a Marxist theorist who adopted a name that means "Long March" (in reference to Mao Zedong's exploits in China), advocated land reforms following the Chinese model, which were ultimately unsuccessful. Finally, **Pham Van Dong** was an able negotiator who often represented the Viet Minh in its dealings with outside groups. The experienced, patient, dedicated leadership of these men made them immensely popular with the Vietnamese peasants—and contrasted sharply with the unpopular, corrupt governments in South Vietnam, both the kingdom of Bao Dai and the U.S.-backed government that would emerge later.

GROUPS IN SOUTH VIETNAM
At the time of the French return to Vietnam, three other important groups in southern Vietnam commanded large followings and

existed outside the Viet Minh influence. The first was the **Cao Dai**, the adherents of an eclectic cult that combined aspects of Eastern religions and Western pop culture. The **Hao Hoa**, meanwhile, combined Buddhism and nationalism and maintained a sizable army. Finally, the **Binh Xuyen**, headquartered in a Chinese-dominated suburb of Saigon called Cholon, were essentially the Vietnamese mafia. All three groups had considerable influence in southern Vietnamese politics, which was extremely factionalized and corrupt.

THE FIRST INDOCHINA WAR

With France's return to Vietnam, the ranks of the Viet Minh swelled, and fighting quickly broke out between French and Viet Minh forces. Almost immediately after the war, the French, who did not recognize Ho Chi Minh's government, set up a rival government in the south. By 1949, when the French reinstalled Bao Dai as figurehead, the two sides had fought to a standstill. The fighting between the French and Viet Minh came to be called the **First Indochina War** and would last for another five years, until 1954.

DIEN BIEN PHU

As the war progressed, the French developed a military strategy based on maintaining fortresses, called "hedgehogs," in DRV territory. The French also developed a strategy that called for the occupation of the outpost of **Dien Bien Phu** in the mountains of northern Vietnam, near the border with Laos. The French would build a large central base there and surround it with three artillery bases, luring Viet Minh forces into assaulting the central base and then destroying them in the crossfire from the artillery bases. French forces took Dien Bien Phu in late 1953 and then put their plan into action.

As expected, the Viet Minh did attack Dien Bien Phu in early 1954, but Viet Minh commander General Vo Nguyen Giap saw through the French plan. He had Vietnamese peasants on bicycles carry components of artillery guns piece by piece into the mountains surrounding Dien Bien Phu, often right under the eyes of French troops. Viet Minh forces then reassembled the artillery pieces in the mountains. Using these strategically placed guns to destroy the French airstrip supplying the central base, Giap launched an offensive with 40,000 troops, and Dien Bien Phu fell to the Viet Minh on May 7, 1954.

Although Dien Bien Phu was a stunning Vietnamese victory, many more Vietnamese actually died than French. Historians are quick to highlight Vo Nguyen Giap's military brilliance, but his vic-

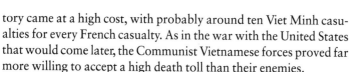

tory came at a high cost, with probably around ten Viet Minh casualties for every French casualty. As in the war with the United States that would come later, the Communist Vietnamese forces proved far more willing to accept a high death toll than their enemies.

THE GENEVA CONFERENCE

The defeat at Dien Bien Phu humiliated the French and turned the tide of French public opinion against the war. The French government, wanting to end the fighting, organized the **Geneva Conference**, which lasted until July 1954. At the conference, diplomats from France, Vietnam, the United States, the USSR, Britain, China, Laos, and Cambodia declared a cease-fire and decided to split Vietnam officially at the **17th parallel**, into Communist-controlled **North Vietnam** (under Ho and the Viet Minh) and **South Vietnam** (under Bao Dai).

The **Geneva Accords**, as these agreements were called, also required French withdrawal from North Vietnam and Viet Minh withdrawal from South Vietnam. The accords also promised reunification of Vietnam after free elections, which were to be to be held by July 1956. As it turned out, these elections were never held.

SUMMARY & ANALYSIS

U.S. INVOLVEMENT AND THE COLD WAR CONTEXT: 1947–1955

EVENTS

1947	Containment doctrine begins to influence U.S. foreign policy
1948	USSR blockades Berlin; United States responds with Berlin airlift
1949	USSR conducts first successful atomic bomb test China falls to Communist rebels under Mao Zedong
1954	Eisenhower articulates domino theory
1955	U.S.-backed Ngo Dinh Diem ousts Bao Dai from power in South Vietnam

KEY PEOPLE

George F. Kennan	U.S. State Department analyst who developed influential policy of containment in 1947
Harry S Truman	33rd U.S. president; adopted containment as a major part of U.S. foreign policy
Dwight D. Eisenhower	34th U.S. president; modified containment policy with more pessimistic domino theory
Ngo Dinh Diem	U.S.–backed leader of South Vietnam; took power in fraudulent elections in 1955
Edward Lansdale	CIA operative stationed in Vietnam in 1954; eventually became advisor to Diem

ORIGINS OF THE COLD WAR

U.S. involvement in Vietnam occurred within and because of the larger context of the **Cold War** between the United States and the Soviet Union. Immediately after World War II, tensions between the United States and USSR escalated, as Soviet forces occupied nearly all of Eastern Europe and set up Communist governments there as a buffer between the Soviet Union and the capitalist West. In 1946, British prime minister **Winston Churchill** famously railed against the USSR in his **"iron curtain"** speech, which lamented the sudden wall of secrecy that had gone up between Eastern and Western Europe.

CONTAINMENT

In 1947, U.S. State Department analyst **George F. Kennan** argued that the USSR was not likely to make any rash moves and that the United States could keep Communism from spreading simply by deterring Soviet expansion at critical points, mostly in Europe, over the long term. This policy of **containment** became extraordinarily influential in the U.S. government and became the basis of U.S. policy for much of the Cold War.

Escalation and Paranoia

Three major events in 1948 and 1949 brought the American fear of Communism to a fever pitch. First, the USSR, which controlled East Germany, attempted to drive U.S., British, and French forces out of West Berlin by cutting off all outside access to the city. The United States responded to this blockade with the **Berlin airlift** over the winter of 1948–1949, dropping crucial supplies into West Berlin until the Soviet Union relented. Then, in August 1949, the USSR successfully tested its first **atomic bomb**. Finally, in October 1949, after years of civil war, the Nationalist government of **China** fell to the Communist forces of **Mao Zedong**. The combined force of these three events plunged the United States into a deep paranoia and fear that Communists would take over the world and might even be plotting secret operations in the United States.

NSC-68

In this environment of alarm, national security advisors of U.S. president **Harry S Truman** wrote an influential memo called **NSC-68**, which advocated a tremendous increase in military spending to finance a massive military buildup, hoping to deter Soviet aggression. Following the policy outlined by this document, the United States became increasingly concerned with Communist expansion anywhere, not just at the critical points that Kennan had identified. Combined with the beginning of the **Korean War** in 1950, NSC-68 encouraged President Truman to begin a rapid buildup of the U.S. military.

The Domino Theory

After the fall of Dien Bien Phu in 1954, Truman's successor, President **Dwight D. Eisenhower**, gave a speech that would soon become famous and important as an outline of U.S. Cold War policy. In the speech, Eisenhower drew on Kennan's previously articulated containment policy but went a step further in describing what became known as the **domino theory**. Eisenhower stated that the United States needed not only to contain the USSR at critical locations but in *all* locations, for if one nation became Communist, its neighbors were likely to turn Communist as well, falling like a row of dominoes.

As a result of the domino theory, U.S. policy makers began to see Vietnam as extremely important. If Vietnam became Communist, domino-theory logic held that all of Indochina, and perhaps even all of Southeast Asia, might become Communist. Well aware of the popularity of Ho Chi Minh and his Viet Minh associates in both North and South Vietnam, U.S. leaders feared that the free elections promised at the Geneva Conference, which were scheduled to occur in 1956, would result in a unified, Communist Vietnam.

NGO DINH DIEM

Committed to the logic of the domino theory, U.S. leaders sought to forestall the elections in Vietnam. The United States thus threw its support behind the politician **Ngo Dinh Diem**, a Vietnamese nationalist and Catholic who emphasized Confucian values of loyalty and tradition and opposed the overthrow of old Vietnamese social structures—a move that the revolutionary Vietnamese Communists advocated.

THE REPUBLIC OF VIETNAM

In 1955, with U.S. support, Diem rejected the prospect of Vietnam-wide elections as specified by the Geneva Accords and instead held a referendum limited to the southern half of the country. Using fraud and intimidation, Diem won over 98 percent of the vote, removed the feeble Bao Dai from power, and proclaimed South Vietnam to be the **Republic of Vietnam (RVN)**. A CIA operative working in Saigon, **Edward Lansdale**, was installed as an advisor to Diem. The United States then helped Diem organize the **Army of the Republic of Vietnam (ARVN)** to control his new state.

ASSESSING U.S. INVOLVEMENT

The United States' involvement in Vietnam can be understood only within the context of the larger Cold War against the Soviet Union. After formulating the policy of containment and the domino theory in a response to the USSR, the United States would become more and more involved in checking Communism's spread in Vietnam. Americans and others around the world had watched as Britain and France appeased Adolf Hitler and the expansionist Nazi Germany prior to World War II—an approach that had quickly brought disaster. As a result, rather than appease the USSR, the United States vowed to stop aggression before it happened. Whether or not this new tactic would work, or was even appropriate, was not yet clear. Policy makers today claim to have learned the "lessons of Vietnam," but the American tragedy in Vietnam was itself largely built on "lessons of World War II."

DIEM AND THE REPUBLIC OF VIETNAM: 1955–1960

EVENTS	
1955	Diem initiates ARVN-enforced land redistribution
1959	Diem regime passes Law 10/59 to root out Communists
1960	South Vietnamese Communists form National Liberation Front

KEY PEOPLE	
Ngo Dinh Diem	U.S.-backed leader of South Vietnam; ran anti-Buddhist regime that was rife with corruption and nepotism
Ngo Dinh Thuc	Diem's brother; also the Catholic archbishop of Hue
Ngo Dinh Nhu	Diem's youngest brother, whom Diem appointed chief of the government's Can Lao secret police organization
Madame Nhu	Nhu's wife; served as South Vietnam's de facto first lady and became wildly controversial

DIEM IN OFFICE

Upon taking office, **Ngo Dinh Diem** quickly developed a reputation for using force rather than democratic means to initiate change. Beginning in 1955, he used **ARVN** troops to reverse Communist land redistribution in South Vietnam and return landholdings to the previous owners. Fearful of Viet Minh popularity and activity in rural areas—which had increased as a result of Diem's cancellation of the scheduled 1956 elections—Diem uprooted villagers from their lands and moved them to settlements under government or army surveillance. He forcibly drafted many of these peasants into ARVN, increasing his unpopularity in rural areas even further.

CATHOLICISM AND NEPOTISM

Diem's government was also unpopular because it had an overwhelming **Catholic** bias and contained several unpopular, key figures who were members of Diem's own family, the Ngo family. Although Catholics made up less than a tenth of the Vietnamese population, Diem himself was Catholic, as were all his other family members in the government. Diem's government engaged in often vicious persecution of **Buddhists**, who made up the overwhelming majority of Vietnamese citizens, particularly peasants. Diem's brother **Ngo Dinh Thuc**, the influential Catholic archbishop of Hue, in particular came into conflict with Buddhists.

Diem continued his nepotistic trend by installing his youngest brother, **Ngo Dinh Nhu**, as the leader of the government's secret police organization, the **Can Lao**. Moreover, because Diem himself was not married, his sister-in-law, Nhu's wildly unpopular, Franco-phile wife, **Madame Nhu**, became South Vietnam's de facto first lady. In the years that followed, Madame Nhu would emerge as a notorious figure in Vietnam and on the world stage; arrogant, extravagant, and prone to nasty, on-the-record comments, she created one public relations disaster after another for the U.S.-backed Diem government.

DIEM'S CRACKDOWN ON COMMUNISM

In general, Diem's repressive policies between 1955 and 1959, though designed to root out Communists from South Vietnam, actually increased sympathy for Communists in the South and swelled the ranks of the southern **Viet Minh**. Although the southern Viet Minh were anxious to revolt against Diem, Viet Minh leaders in the North held back their southern forces because they feared that the United States might get involved in the conflict.

In May 1959, Diem passed **Law 10/59**, establishing military tribunals to search out Communists in South Vietnam, whom he derisively referred to as **Viet Cong**. These tribunals were unconcerned with justice, and Law 10/59 was brutal in its application.

THE NATIONAL LIBERATION FRONT

In 1960, a group of Vietnamese intellectuals issued the **Caravelle Manifesto**, which called for mild reforms to Diem's corrupt regime. Diem, paranoid, unable to take criticism, and unwilling to negotiate, threw the reformers in jail and refused to diminish the power of his much-hated brother Nhu. A coup against Diem was attempted later that year but failed.

Also in 1960, in an effort to present a united front, southern Communists formed the **National Liberation Front (NLF)**, which the North Vietnamese government officially recognized and sanctioned. Immediately, the NLF began a program to both train and arm guerrilla soldiers. Over the course of the next few years, the terms "NLF" and "Viet Cong" began to be used interchangeably, and ultimately the once-derisive "Viet Cong" became common parlance that was used throughout the war, especially by the U.S. military.

ASSESSING DIEM'S REGIME

Although the Ngo family was universally hated in South Vietnam, Diem, despite his Catholic faith and dictatorial tendencies, had been widely respected as a sincere nationalist in the years before he came to power. Indeed, he was in many respects just as nationalistic as Ho Chi Minh. It was for these reasons that the United States felt that

Diem represented the best hope for a strong South Vietnamese government that could resist Communist influence.

As it turned out, Diem's regime was undemocratic, corrupt, and extreme from the beginning, and, as evidenced by the formation of ARVN, dependent on U.S. strength. Though Diem was popular among Catholics and had some influence in South Vietnam's cities, his regime was universally hated in rural areas, which proved a perfect hiding and training ground for Communist forces. And in a nation as undeveloped as Vietnam was at the time, power in the cities meant far less than it would have in a developed country.

Indeed, though the United States established Diem as leader to halt Communist expansion, his repressive techniques, corrupt government, and inept public relations—such as his decision to grant his hated sister-in-law, Madame Nhu, a public stage—had the opposite effect. Under Diem, the number of active southern Communists increased dramatically. To the United States, operating under the domino theory, this Communist expansion posed a massive threat.

SUMMARY & ANALYSIS

KENNEDY AND THE FIRST U.S. INVOLVEMENT: 1961–1963

EVENTS

1960	USSR begins airlifting to Communist Pathet Lao forces in Laos
1961	Kennedy takes office
1962	United States (MACV); sends first "military advisors" to Vietnam Cuban Missile Crisis increases Cold War tensions
1963	Battle of Ap Bac sees Viet Cong forces rout ARVN Buddhist monk immolates himself in protest of Diem's policies Diem overthrown in U.S.-backed coup Kennedy assassinated; Johnson becomes president

KEY PEOPLE

John F. Kennedy	35th U.S. president; sent "military advisors" to Vietnam under auspices of MACV; assassinated in 1963
Robert S. McNamara	Kennedy's secretary of defense; also served under Johnson
McGeorge Bundy	Kennedy's national security advisor; advocated early escalation of U.S. involvement in Vietnam
Ngo Dinh Diem	U.S.-backed leader of South Vietnam; deposed and executed by ARVN coup in 1963
Madame Nhu	De facto first lady of South Vietnam; caused outrage by dismissing a Buddhist monk's self-immolation in protest of the Diem regime as a "barbecuing"
Duong Van Minh	ARVN general who became leader of South Vietnam after ouster of Diem
Lyndon B. Johnson	Vice president under Kennedy; became president after Kennedy's assassination in 1963

THE KENNEDY ADMINISTRATION

In November 1960, the young Massachusetts senator **John F. Kennedy** was elected U.S. president. When he took office in January 1961, his administration portrayed itself as a break from the older traditions and as the "best and brightest," with former Rhodes Scholar **Dean Rusk** as secretary of state, renowned businessman **Robert S. McNamara** as secretary of defense, and academic **McGeorge Bundy** as national security advisor. The president also appointed his brother, Robert F. Kennedy, as attorney general. This group would remain Kennedy's key advisors, especially in matters relating to Vietnam, throughout his entire time in office.

Despite Kennedy's attempts to appear tough on Communism, Soviet premier **Nikita Khrushchev** suspected that the young president would be more easily intimated than his predecessor, Eisenhower, who had been one of the major Allied military commanders in

World War II. In the young and inexperienced Kennedy, Khrushchev saw an opportunity to press for strategic gains.

LAOS AND CUBA

In 1960, the Soviet Union began airlifting supplies to the Pathet Lao, a Communist-led group of guerrilla insurgents fighting against the French in Vietnam's neighboring country, **Laos**. U.S. policy makers worried that the first domino in Indochina was about to fall, and for a brief time, small, landlocked Laos became an important locale in the global Cold War confrontation between the world's two superpowers.

Then, in 1962, Khrushchev upped the stakes even further by placing Soviet nuclear warheads on the Communist-governed island of **Cuba**, just ninety miles from the United States. Kennedy, proving himself a master of brinkmanship, ordered the U.S. Navy to blockade Cuba and refused to back down. Ultimately, it was Khrushchev himself who backed down, removing the missiles in exchange for U.S. concessions. Although the **Cuban Missile Crisis** ended peacefully, it brought tensions to the highest point yet seen in the Cold War.

"MILITARY ADVISORS" AND THE MACV

Within this context of increased conflict, the United States in 1962 established the **Military Assistance Command of Vietnam (MACV)**, which provided American personnel to help train the South Vietnamese army, the **ARVN**, in its growing conflicts with Communist guerrillas. Under the auspices of the MACV, the United States sent thousands of **"military advisors"** to South Vietnam; within a year, the American presence rose from around 1,000 men to over 15,000. Although the U.S. government maintained that these "military advisors" were not "military forces" per se, the line quickly became quite blurred.

Moreover, in a major embarrassment for the United States, many of the 250,000 weapons that the MACV distributed to the ARVN that year likely ended up in the hands of the **Viet Cong**. In fact, many ARVN soldiers who had been drafted from the ranks of the peasants were also secretly members of the National Liberation Front at the same time. In short, the MACV not only drastically escalated the U.S. presence in Vietnam but also spent a good deal of time and money training the enemy.

"STRATEGIC HAMLETS"

Because Viet Cong forces and ARVN forces often lived in the same villages and undercover Viet Cong members were widespread, air power was a largely useless tool in the fight to extricate Communists from South Vietnam. For this reason, MACV decided that South Vietnamese peasants should be relocated into fortified **"strategic hamlets,"** allowing U.S. and ARVN forces not only to protect these peasants but also to try to label the Viet Cong as anyone *not* living in a strategic hamlet. Unfortunately, the MACV entrusted the job of constructing these strategic hamlets to the much-hated **Ngo Dinh Nhu**, under whose direction the hamlets were run essentially as labor camps. As peasants in the hamlets grew angry at these conditions, many defected to the Viet Cong side.

MEDIA COVERAGE

The year 1963 marked a turning point, both because the first clashes of the nascent war emerged and because American **news coverage** of Vietnam began to slip toward pessimism. Unlike prior coverage, which had come largely in the form of positive "headway reports," media coverage in 1963 began to reveal serious problems to the American public.

At one of the first major battles between ARVN and Viet Cong forces, the **Battle of Ap Bac** in January 1963, a vastly outnumbered and outgunned Viet Cong force nonetheless inflicted more casualties on the ARVN than vice versa. The official U.S. report claimed that the battle was an important victory for the anti-Communist forces, but two American journalists on the scene reported that the battle was a rout against the ARVN and postulated that U.S. involvement in Vietnam might quickly become a quagmire. As it turned out, the journalists' words were prophetic, and the battle itself was emblematic of the way much of the war would go.

BUDDHIST PROTESTORS AND MADAME NHU

Meanwhile, the corruption and brutality of the Diem government against Vietnam's **Buddhist** leaders continued and soon caused a major crisis. In May 1963, ARVN troops fired on a group of Buddhist protesters in the city of **Hue**, where Diem's brother **Ngo Dinh Thuc** reigned as archbishop. The next month, a Buddhist monk doused himself in gasoline and burned himself to death in protest, in public and in full view of a number of journalists.

Pictures of this self-immolation made the front pages of world newspapers the next day and provoked outrage against the Diem

regime. South Vietnam's "first lady," **Madame Nhu**, only worsened Diem's image by publicly dismissing the incident as a "barbecuing," deriding the monk for using "imported gasoline," and offering to provide fuel and matches for the next monk who wanted to follow suit.

THE END OF THE DIEM REGIME

In August 1963, dissatisfied with the Diem regime in general and Diem's brother Nhu in particular, ARVN generals began a new plot to overthrow Diem. This time, the effort was secretly backed by CIA operatives and the U.S. ambassador in Saigon. On November 1, the coup was carried out, and General **Duong Van Minh** took power. Diem and his brother Nhu were both executed. The new military rulers proved unstable, and in the period that followed, South Vietnam had little consistent leadership.

KENNEDY'S ASSASSINATION

On November 22, 1963, just three weeks after Diem's assassination in Saigon, President Kennedy was assassinated in Dallas. Vice President **Lyndon B. Johnson** was sworn into office, kept Kennedy's key Vietnam advisors in place, and pledged, "Let us continue." The United States would soon be well past the point of no return in Vietnam.

THE RESULTS OF KENNEDY'S POLICIES

Despite Kennedy's talented advisors, his administration made policy mistakes in Vietnam that led the United States into deeper involvement. The strategic hamlet program was an utter failure: it not only failed to root out Viet Cong influence but actually made it stronger, as Nhu's mismanagement turned many of the 4.3 million peasants forced into the hamlets against the Diem regime and toward the Communist side. The U.S. decision to allow Diem's overthrow after years of support, though likely necessary, revealed the United States as the true power operating behind the scenes and robbed the South Vietnamese government of whatever shreds of authority it still maintained.

Moreover, the American media's quick exposure of these bungled U.S. actions marked the first time that journalists had ever played such an immediate "fact-checking" role in a U.S. conflict. Until 1963, Americans had received news only of Diem's popularity and successes. But after the Battle of Ap Bac and the Buddhist monk's self-immolation, the American media began to present an increasingly critical view of U.S. policy in Vietnam.

This shift had a profound impact on public opinion: the American people slowly turned against the war, and protest movements grew in strength (*see* The U.S. Antiwar Movement, *p. 49*). On a larger level, the media's role in Vietnam prompted an evolution toward more cynical media coverage of the U.S. government in general—a trend of increased media scrutiny that has continued up to the present day.

JOHNSON AND ESCALATION: 1964–1966

EVENTS

August 1964	U.S. destroyers in Gulf of Tonkin report North Vietnamese attacks U.S. Congress passes Gulf of Tonkin Resolution
November 1964	Johnson wins presidential election
February 1965	Pleiku Raid kills eight U.S. soldiers U.S. forces begin Operation Rolling Thunder bombing campaign
June 1965	United States reaches 75,000 troops in Vietnam
July 1965	Johnson authorizes an additional 100,000 troops, allocates 100,000 more for 1966
November 1965	Battle of Ia Drang

KEY PEOPLE

Lyndon B. Johnson	36th U.S. president; escalated U.S. troop levels in Vietnam drastically after Gulf of Tonkin incident
Barry M. Goldwater	Hawkish senator from Arizona who ran unsuccessfully against Johnson in 1964 election
William C. Westmoreland	U.S. general who advocated aggressive strategies against Viet Cong and NVA using large numbers of U.S. forces
Ho Chi Minh	North Vietnamese Communist leader; used guerrilla tactics to prolong the war and frustrate U.S. forces

THE JOHNSON ADMINISTRATION

New president **Lyndon B. Johnson** inherited a difficult situation in Vietnam, as the South Vietnamese government was in shambles and the Viet Cong was making large gains in rural areas of the South. Although Johnson billed himself as a tough anti-Communist, he pledged to honor Kennedy's limited troop commitments in Vietnam. Indeed, Johnson handled the Vietnam situation moderately during the early part of his term, striving to continue Kennedy's programs without dramatically escalating the war.

NEW STRATEGIES

Johnson did make several changes in U.S. military leadership. Although **Robert S. McNamara** remained as secretary of defense, General **Earle G. Wheeler** became the new chairman of the Joint Chiefs of Staff. General **William C. Westmoreland** was instated as commander of the MACV, replacing previous commander General Paul Harkins, by then referred to as "General Blimp" for his tendency to inflate the ARVN's successes.

Westmoreland, disgusted with the corruption and incompetence of the ARVN, pushed for 200,000 American ground troops. Meanwhile, National Security Advisor **McGeorge Bundy** argued for increased bombing of targets in North Vietnam, especially factories. McNamara, a student of game theory, advocated a "tit-for-tat" policy against North Vietnam, in which U.S. forces would strike Hanoi every time the Viet Cong went on the offensive in South Vietnam.

THE GULF OF TONKIN INCIDENT

Despite these suggestions, Johnson maintained a moderate policy until August 1964, when the situation changed dramatically. Early that month, two U.S. Navy destroyers in the **Gulf of Tonkin** (off the coast of North Vietnam) reported that North Vietnamese gunboats attacked them unprovoked. The American public was incensed, and Johnson requested from Congress the authority to take "all necessary steps" to protect U.S. interests in Vietnam. Congress complied and passed the **Gulf of Tonkin Resolution** in August 1964. Out of the 535 total members of Congress, only two voted against this resolution, which policy makers considered a declaration of war in everything but name. Indeed, Johnson ordered bombing runs on North Vietnam not long after the incident.

Soon after the resolution was passed, a debate emerged over the nature of the attacks on the U.S. ships in the Gulf of Tonkin. Many have argued that the second attack did not occur at all. Others have argued that the attacks were not entirely unprovoked, as the U.S. ships were likely involved in covert missions against North Vietnam that were unknown to the American public at the time. Nonetheless, the U.S. government embraced the public's anger about the attacks and ultimately used it as a justification to escalate the war.

JOHNSON'S REELECTION

Although Johnson deferred openly escalating the war until after the election of 1964, the furor over the Gulf of Tonkin incident only helped Johnson in his campaign. His hawkish Republican opponent, **Barry M. Goldwater**, argued that much more needed to be done in Vietnam to contain Communism. Johnson countered by touting his "Great Society" program for domestic reform and by airing the famous "Daisy Girl" political commercial, which played on the American public's fears that Goldwater's aggressiveness might start a nuclear war. Johnson also promised that his government would not "supply American boys to do the job that Asian boys should do." On Election Day, Johnson won by a landslide.

INSTABILITY IN SOUTH VIETNAM

Meanwhile, South Vietnam, lacking the order that Diem's dictatorial regime provided, had become increasingly chaotic. Although ARVN general **Nguyen Khanh** emerged from the leadership vacuum as a figurehead of sorts, he too proved ineffective, and riots against him broke out in November 1964. After a February 1965 coup, **Nguyen Van Thieu** and **Nguyen Cao Ky** succeeded him. Ky was a swaggering, beer-swilling military man who styled himself as Vietnam's John Wayne. U.S. officials tried to control him by making the more conservative Thieu chief executive, but both men were so deeply involved in the rampant corruption in South Vietnam that their leadership was not what the country needed.

OPERATION ROLLING THUNDER

By 1965, **Viet Cong** attacks on U.S. forces were becoming increasingly violent, and though the Viet Cong obviously had many soldiers in South Vietnam, the MACV was still having difficulty locating any bombing targets at all. In February 1965, Viet Cong guerrillas attacked a U.S. Marine barracks at the South Vietnamese hamlet of **Pleiku**, killing eight and wounding over a hundred others.

With the free hand recently provided by Congress, Johnson ordered the U.S. Air Force and U.S. Navy to begin an intense series of air strikes called **Operation Rolling Thunder**. He hoped that the bombing campaign would demonstrate to the South Vietnamese the U.S. commitment to their cause and its resolve to halt the spread of Communism. Ironically, the air raids seemed only to increase the number of Viet Cong and NVA (North Vietnamese Army) attacks.

"AMERICANIZATION"

Despite Johnson's campaign promise to keep "American boys" out of Vietnam, Operation Rolling Thunder set the gears in motion for a major escalation of the war, culminating in the first arrival of U.S. ground troops in 1965. General Westmoreland, doubting the corrupt and ineffective ARVN's ability to defend U.S. air bases against the Viet Cong, lobbied successfully for two Marine battalions to protect the base at **Da Nang**. For the first time, U.S. ground troops—not just MACV advisors—were committed to Vietnam. The war was undergoing **"Americanization."**

THE ENCLAVE STRATEGY

Johnson, meanwhile, advocated an inconsistent strategy: although at one point in 1965 he promised North Vietnamese leader **Ho Chi Minh** "unconditional discussions," he also harbored a belief that a gradual increase in the U.S. military presence in Vietnam would make Ho more willing to negotiate and perhaps even cause him to withdraw NVA troops from South Vietnam. The United States did send more troops, and a total of 75,000 were in Vietnam by June 1965, just ten months after the Gulf of Tonkin Resolution.

With these troops in place, U.S. officials instituted an **"enclave" strategy** under which U.S. forces would try to maintain only those areas of Vietnam already under Saigon's control. General Westmoreland, opposing the enclave strategy, called for more and more U.S. forces and advocated "taking the battle to the enemy." Indeed, in July 1965, Johnson sent 100,000 more troops and authorized another 100,000 to be dispatched in 1966.

Continued Bombing Campaigns

Throughout 1965, the U.S. military continued its bombing campaigns, so heavily that by the end of the decade it had dropped 3 million tons of bombs on Vietnam—more than all the bombs dropped in Europe during World War II. Despite the enormous number of bombs used, the campaign had little effect. Target selection was difficult against the hidden Viet Cong and rural, non-industrialized North Vietnamese. Moreover, Ho Chi Minh decided to evacuate much of the population of Hanoi in order to give Rolling Thunder still fewer targets. Nonetheless, the United States continued bombing in an attempt to demoralize the North Vietnamese, misunderstanding both the commitment of the Communist nationalists and the terrain of Vietnam.

A War of Attrition

In 1965, Westmoreland began to implement a **search-and-destroy** strategy that sent U.S. troops out into the field to find and kill Viet Cong members. Westmoreland was confident that American technology would succeed in slowly wearing down the Viet Cong through a **war of attrition**—a strategy of extended combat meant to inflict so many casualties on the enemy that it could no longer continue. U.S. leaders agreed, believing that North Vietnam's economy could not sustain a prolonged war effort.

In light of this new strategy of fighting a war of attrition, U.S. commanders were instructed to begin keeping **body counts** of enemy soldiers killed. Although body counts were indeed tallied, they were often exaggerated and proved wildly inaccurate, as the bodies of

Viet Cong soldiers often were difficult to distinguish from the bodies of friendly South Vietnamese soldiers.

Ia Drang

In November 1965, Westmoreland found justification for his search-and-destroy strategy in the **Battle of Ia Drang**, fought in a highland valley in central Vietnam. One of the largest battles of the war, Ia Drang was a damaging loss for the North Vietnamese. The battle simultaneously convinced Westmoreland that his strategy of attrition through search and destroy would work and the North Vietnamese that they should return to their strategy of **guerrilla warfare**, choosing battles only on their own terms. As it turned out, America's top military minds—which had been trained in a tradition of conventional warfare, such as the massive troop movements and invasions of World War II—would indeed have great difficulty fighting a guerrilla war.

The Ho Chi Minh Trail

Meanwhile, U.S. forces continued to try to cut off Viet Cong supply lines through air power. These efforts expended a great deal of time and resources, but the North Vietnamese government proved extremely savvy in its ability to keep the Viet Cong supplied. Rather than attempt to send materials across the heavily guarded **DMZ** (the demilitarized zone surrounding the border between North and South Vietnam at the 17th parallel), they sent supplies via the **Ho Chi Minh Trail**, which ran from North Vietnam through Laos and Cambodia into South Vietnam. Troops and supplies streamed into South Vietnam via the trail, and despite intense U.S. bombing throughout 1965, the trail never closed once, not even temporarily.

North Vietnam's Strategy

In the fight against the United States, Ho Chi Minh and Vo Nguyen Giap (still Ho's top general) followed the same three-phase strategy that had worked against the French. In the first phase, Ho and his forces focused on mere survival and building up a support base. Then, in the second phase, they moved to guerrilla warfare, utilizing small groups of fighters behind enemy lines, placing booby traps, and making small ambushes. This phase, which had frustrated the French enormously, could be maintained for years, as the Viet Cong could disappear into the jungle and their extensive tunnel systems whenever the enemy tried to confront them directly.

SUMMARY & ANALYSIS

The Battle of Ia Drang marked the North's attempt to start their third phase, a "general counteroffensive" that Ho hoped would spark rebellion against imperialists throughout Vietnam. Although Ia Drang resulted in a significant defeat for the North Vietnamese, the eventual Tet Offensive of 1968 (*see* The Tet Offensive, *p. 45*), would be far more effective.

VIET CONG RESILIENCE

Arguably, the United States' main problem in Vietnam was not poor strategy but rather the fact that it greatly underestimated Viet Cong tenacity. Although U.S. leaders did indeed make a series of bad decisions in Vietnam, not every aspect of the U.S. strategy was unsound. Westmoreland's war of attrition, for instance, did in fact have significant impact. However, the Viet Cong's tenacity enabled it to draw the war out into a prolonged guerrilla conflict that the United States was ill equipped to deal with. Rather than hold permanent positions and fight along conventional lines, the Viet Cong harassed U.S. troops incessantly in small groups, striking quickly and then disappearing into the jungle or the peasant population. With this dogged strategy, even a poor, third world nation was able to make significant headway against the world's leading military superpower.

TWO DIFFERENT WARS

The Viet Cong's tenacity stemmed from its nationalistic motivations, which were quite different from the United States' objectives in Vietnam—in effect, the Americans and North Vietnamese were fighting two entirely different wars. From the American viewpoint, Vietnam was just another pawn in the great Cold War chess game.

Though U.S. leaders claimed they were defending democracy in South Vietnam, this claim was mostly false. The South Vietnamese "democracy" was largely a U.S.-created fiction in the first place; the U.S.-backed regime under Ngo Dinh Diem had been brutal, corrupt, and not even remotely a democracy. As a result, though Johnson claimed repeatedly that winning the "hearts and minds" of the Vietnamese people was key to winning the war, U.S. policy only alienated the Vietnamese further and further. Privately, U.S. policy makers generally saw themselves as fighting the Soviet Union through the proxy of North Vietnam and the Viet Cong. Vietnam thus was largely a symbolic prize that U.S. leaders wanted to prevent from falling embarrassingly into the Soviet Bloc. Moreover, having propped up Diem, U.S. policy makers were quick to assume that Ho

Chi Minh was similarly just a Sino-Soviet puppet and not a real nationalist leader.

In reality, Ho was much more than simply a puppet: he saw himself and his Communist forces as fighting a heroic, centuries-long crusade to finally push out foreign invaders and reunite their homeland. Indeed, this was, and remained, North Vietnam's military objective all along. Ho stated repeatedly that peace would come only after U.S. troops had left Vietnam, U.S. bombing raids stopped, the NLF was allowed to participate in South Vietnamese politics, and North and South were reunified. For this reason, the Viet Cong, simultaneously Communists and nationalists, would pay any price to keep their hope of independence and a unified Vietnam alive. They were always willing to accept higher casualties and costs than their American opponents, and this gave them a distinct advantage. For this reason, although more than ten Viet Cong soldiers were dying for each U.S. soldier killed, Americans felt themselves to be losing the war while Ho and his followers smelled victory. The fact that U.S. objectives were rather undefined did not help American morale. Though U.S. forces were fighting for victory, it was unclear what victory constituted; for Ho and his forces, the goal was concrete and seemed increasingly within reach.

SUMMARY & ANALYSIS

QUAGMIRE AND THE TET OFFENSIVE: 1966–1968

EVENTS

January 1967	United States reaches nearly 400,000 troops in Vietnam
June 1967	CIA initiates Phoenix Program
January 1968	NVA attacks U.S. Marine base at Khe Sanh North Vietnamese launch Tet Offensive
February 1968	McNamara resigns as secretary of defense
March 1968	Westmoreland causes uproar by requesting 200,000 more troops U.S. soldiers kill 500 Vietnamese civilians in My Lai Massacre

KEY PEOPLE

Lyndon B. Johnson	36th U.S. president; insistence that the United States was winning the war in Vietnam led to the development of the "credibility gap"
Robert McNamara	Johnson's secretary of defense; had initially supported escalation but began to question U.S. involvement and resigned in early 1968
William C. Westmoreland	Commander of U.S. military in Vietnam; made enormous political blunder by requesting Congress for 200,000 more troops after Tet Offensive of 1968
William Calley	U.S. Army lieutenant in charge of company that killed 500 Vietnamese civilians at My Lai; was court-martialed in 1971 but paroled in 1974

SUMMARY & ANALYSIS

CHANGING STRATEGIES

By 1966, both sides in the Vietnam War started changing their strategies. General **Nguyen Chi Thanh**, a top Viet Cong commander, began to push for a general offensive. Meanwhile, General **William C. Westmoreland**'s search-and-destroy operations were fully under way. Although many of Westmoreland's campaigns were successful in killing Viet Cong forces, they also required large numbers of U.S. troops.

By the end of 1966, nearly 400,000 U.S. soldiers were in Vietnam; this number would reach 500,000 by the end of 1968. President Johnson also authorized the use of chemical weapons such as **napalm**, a thick gasoline-based gel that can be sprayed and burns at high temperatures, and **Agent Orange**, a chemical defoliant that was used to destroy jungle vegetation to expose Viet Cong hideouts. Although both of these weapons were effective, they inflicted horrific devastation, and Agent Orange in particular caused unforeseen health problems among both troops and Vietnamese civilians, the effects of which have persisted for decades.

THE COSVN

In late 1966, U.S. forces began to search for the so-called Central Office of South Vietnam, or **COSVN**—the Viet Cong command center that U.S. officials insisted existed somewhere in the jungle, directing Viet Cong operations throughout Vietnam. The existence of the COSVN has never been confirmed, however, and it is likely there never really was such a command center at all. Nonetheless, General Westmoreland initiated a series of search campaigns in the so-called **Iron Triangle**, a sixty-square-mile area north of Saigon. Although several thousand Viet Cong were killed in a campaign that lasted until 1967, U.S. forces failed to locate COSVN or make any progress in encircling or rooting out the Viet Cong.

THE "CREDIBILITY GAP"

Despite the numerous setbacks, Johnson and other U.S. officials, citing increased troop numbers and redefined objectives, again claimed to be making headway in the war. Photos and video footage of dead American soldiers in newspapers and on evening news programs, however, indicated otherwise. Moreover, U.S. spending in support of the war had reached record levels, costing the government an estimated $3 billion a month. As a result, many people in the United States began to speak of a **"credibility gap"** between what Johnson and the U.S. government were telling the American people and what actually was transpiring on the ground.

KHE SANH

Throughout 1967, Viet Cong guerrillas stepped up their attacks on U.S. servicemen. Then, in late January 1968, the North Vietnamese Army launched a major offensive against the U.S. Marine base at **Khe Sanh**, just below the DMZ. U.S. commanders, determined to hold the base, sent 50,000 men as reinforcements. Though one of the largest battles of the war, Khe Sanh was essentially a diversion planned by the Viet Cong in an effort to weaken American forces farther south, paving the way for a more significant offensive.

THE TET OFFENSIVE

Indeed, with U.S. forces still north at Khe Sanh, the Viet Cong launched the **Tet Offensive**, the large "general offensive" that Ho Chi Minh and the Vietnamese Communists had been planning for years. On January 30, 1968, on the Vietnamese new year holiday of Tet, separate Viet Cong and NVA cells attacked twenty-seven different U.S. military installations throughout South Vietnam at the same time.

Fighting was intense, but U.S. forces managed to kill or capture the bulk of the Viet Cong raiders within several weeks. The toughest combat occurred in the city of **Hue**, which the NVA actually conquered for a few weeks before U.S. troops took it back. Fighting occurred as far south as **Saigon**, taking over the streets. Amid the chaos, an Associated Press photographer captured South Vietnam's chief of police, **Nguyen Ngoc Loan**, executing a Viet Cong captain in the streets of Saigon—a brutal image that shocked the American public and became a symbol of the Vietnam quagmire.

EFFECTS OF THE TET OFFENSIVE

Although the Tet Offensive was quashed relatively quickly, it was an enormous political defeat for the U.S. Army and for Johnson because it proved, despite Johnson's pronouncements, that the war was far from over. The attack not only turned millions of Americans against the war but also split the Democratic Party and the entire U.S. government into antiwar and pro-war factions. In February 1968, Johnson's own secretary of defense, **Robert McNamara**, resigned.

In March, when General Westmoreland and the leaders of the Joint Chiefs of Staff requested 200,000 more soldiers be sent to Vietnam, the American public and policy makers alike were dumbfounded. Westmoreland's request in turn prompted many foreign policy officials, including former secretary of state **Dean Acheson**, to denounce the army's strategy of victory by attrition. Johnson ultimately denied Westmoreland the additional troops.

One of the great ironies of the war was the fact that the Tet Offensive was actually a resounding tactical victory for the United States. The NVA gained no territory for more than a brief period, while 40,000 Vietnamese Communist troops died compared to about 3,000 Americans and South Vietnamese combined. The Tet Offensive thus severely damaged Ho Chi Minh's armies. Nonetheless, the cost in terms of U.S. public opinion would far outweigh the military victory.

WORSENING PUBLIC OPINION

In February 1968, American journalist **Walter Cronkite** famously commented on the CBS Evening News that the United States was mired in a stalemate and that the war probably could not be won. Indeed, the American public, which had long been reassured that the U.S. military was making progress, felt betrayed after the Tet Offensive. Over 500,000 U.S. troops were stationed in Vietnam, and nearly 30,000 had been killed, all in the name of a vaguely defined war that seemed suddenly unwinnable. No longer willing or able to straddle the widening credibility gap, Johnson announced at the end of March that he would not run for reelection in the 1968 election.

Waning Morale

The Tet Offensive also took a significant toll on **morale** among U.S. troops. With the apparent military victory of the offensive undermined by eroding support at home and a seeming lack of military goals or ideas, American soldiers became increasingly upset and disillusioned by the war. Drug abuse among American soldiers was growing rampant, and even cases of **"fragging,"** in which soldiers killed their own superior officers in order to avoid being sent on missions, began to appear.

The My Lai Massacre

This discontentment among U.S. troops resulted in one of the most horrible incidents of the war, in March 1968. Soldiers in one U.S. company, frustrated at their inability to find Viet Cong during a search-and-destroy mission in the tiny South Vietnamese village of My Lai, killed approximately 500 unarmed Vietnamese civilians, including women, children, and elderly. The **My Lai Massacre** was covered up and did not become public knowledge until late 1969. In 1971, Lieutenant **William Calley**, commander of the company, was sentenced to life imprisonment for war crimes. Despite shock at the massacre, however, many in the American felt that Calley was a scapegoat for wider problems, and he was released on parole in 1974.

The Phoenix Program

After the Tet Offensive, the U.S. government stepped up its **covert operations**, the most famous of which was the CIA-led **Phoenix Program**, which had been initiated in June 1967. Among other objectives, the program was meant to assassinate Viet Cong leadership. Although approximately 20,000 people were assassinated under the Phoenix Program, the program was plagued by corruption, mismanagement, and faulty intelligence, and many of its victims were likely not Viet Cong at all. In many cases, unscrupulous South Vietnamese officials named their opponents as Viet Cong and requested that the Phoenix Program eliminate them. When the details of the program later surfaced, many protested that its activities amounted to nothing more than war crimes.

THE U.S. ELECTION OF 1968

Johnson's early withdrawal from the 1968 U.S. presidential race allowed other Democrats to step in, including two antiwar candidates from the Senate, **Eugene McCarthy** and **Robert F. Kennedy**, and Johnson's pro-war vice president, **Hubert Humphrey**. Kennedy, the younger brother of former president John F. Kennedy, seemed sure to win the party's nomination until he was assassinated at a Los Angeles hotel in June 1968. Humphrey became the Democratic nominee instead. However, violence outside the **Democratic National Convention** in Chicago (*see* The Chicago Riot and Kent State, *p. 50*) ruined Humphrey's chances, as American voters erroneously linked the police brutality with the Democratic Party.

Republicans capitalized on the riot and nominated Eisenhower's former vice president, **Richard M. Nixon**, on a pro-war platform. Alabama governor **George C. Wallace** also ran as a third-party candidate, for the war and against civil rights. Because the riot had tainted Humphrey's public image and because Wallace seemed far too conservative, Nixon won the election easily.

The U.S. Antiwar Movement: 1960–1970

EVENTS	
1959	Students for a Democratic Society is founded
1965	First draft riots occur on college campuses
1966	Fulbright publishes *The Arrogance of Power*
1967	Johnson authorizes CIA to investigate antiwar activists 35,000 protesters demonstrate outside the Pentagon
1968	Protest outside Democratic National Convention turns violent
1970	National Guard kills four protesters at Kent State University

KEY PEOPLE	
Lyndon B. Johnson	36th U.S. president; used the FBI to track and detain antiwar protesters
Richard M. Nixon	37th U.S. president; claimed existence of "silent majority" of Americans who supported the war
J. William Fulbright	Arkansas senator who criticized Johnson and U.S. war strategy in Senate hearings in 1966

SUMMARY & ANALYSIS

The Student Movement

By the time of the Tet Offensive, the **antiwar movement** in the United States had been in full swing for quite some time. The 1960s in the United States were already a quasi-revolutionary period: the civil rights movement had flourished under Martin Luther King Jr. and other black leaders, and the post–World War II "baby boom" had produced an especially large youth generation, who thanks to post-war prosperity were attending college in large numbers. Not surprisingly, a large **student protest movement** emerged as U.S. involvement in Vietnam grew.

In 1959, students had founded the semi-socialist **Students for a Democratic Society (SDS)**. Many students at universities across the country held **"teach-in"** rallies, which quickly transformed into pro-test marches as the war progressed. By 1965, after the Gulf of Tonkin Resolution, the SDS began to organize protest rallies against the Vietnam **draft**, and some students publicly burned their draft cards. Thousands of young **draft dodgers** fled to Canada and other countries to escape military service.

Hippies and the Counterculture

In many respects, the student antiwar movement reflected growing disillusionment among young Americans about politics and society as a whole. Influenced by the writers of the rebellious **Beat Generation** of the 1950s, young people in the United States expressed frustration about racism, gender issues, consumerism, and authority in general. Many voices in this emergent **counterculture** of the mid- to late 1960s challenged conventional social norms by embracing sex, drugs, and rock-and-roll music.

These **hippies** and so-called **flower children** won the support of a surprising number of academics, including the sociologist **Alfred Kinsey**, who intellectualized the **sexual revolution**. The counterculture movement reached its peak in August 1969, when about 400,000 people descended on the **Woodstock Music and Art Festival** at a farm in upstate New York. With its combination of rock music and radical hippie politics, drug culture and free love, Woodstock became a symbol of the antiwar movement and an expression of the American youth counterculture of the 1960s in general.

ANTIWAR SENTIMENT IN THE PUBLIC

Although the student and hippie movements were the most visible antiwar efforts, concern about Vietnam was certainly not limited to college campuses. As early as 1965, a Gallup Poll showed the war to be the number-one national issue among the American public in general. Prominent Arkansas senator **J. William Fulbright** added fuel to the fire when he published his antiwar and anti-Johnson book *The Arrogance of Power* in 1966. He also chaired a series of nationally televised hearings in the Senate Foreign Relations Committee in 1966, even calling in **George F. Kennan**, who originated the concept of containment, to voice opposition to the war.

THE CIA AND COINTELPRO

In 1967, in an attempt to stem the growing protest movements, President **Lyndon B. Johnson** authorized the **CIA** to investigate prominent antiwar activists, even though the CIA could legally spy only on foreigners. In addition, Johnson ordered the FBI to use its counterintelligence program, **COINTELPRO,** to monitor activists as well. Loyal FBI agents assigned to COINTELPRO arrested many protesters without legal cause or on phony conspiracy charges. Johnson's illegal use of these government security agencies against U.S. citizens angered many and only worsened public discontentment about the war.

THE CHICAGO RIOT AND KENT STATE

As the war dragged on, antiwar marches and protests intensified and at times became violent. At the **Democratic National Convention** in Chicago in August 1968, thousands of city police officers attacked antiwar protesters gathered outside the convention hall with billy clubs and tear gas. The most infamous and tragic incident occurred in early May 1970 at **Kent State University** in Ohio, where National Guard troops called in to calm the scene ended up firing on a crowd, killing four students. The killings touched off protests at hundreds of college campuses across the United States; many of these also turned violent, and two more students were killed in mid-May at **Jackson State University** in Mississippi.

The "Silent Majority"

Inevitably, an anti-antiwar movement developed as pro-war **"hawks"** tried to counter the antiwar **"doves."** In the face of the growing din of antiwar activists, President **Richard M. Nixon** claimed in a November 1969 speech that antiwar protesters constituted merely a small but vocal minority that was attempting to drown out the **"silent majority"** of Americans who did not harbor such "fervent" antiwar sentiments.

In May 1970, just days after the Kent State shootings, a group of construction workers in New York City broke up a student antiwar demonstration, beating up a number of students and storming City Hall. Not long after this **Hard Hat Riot**, another rally in the city drew 100,000 people to protest against the students, whom they saw as wealthy, spoiled brats who were busy protesting while working-class, non–college educated young Americans were dying in Vietnam.

Impact of the Antiwar Movement

The enormous opposition that the Vietnam War provoked was virtually unprecedented in U.S. history and created an antiwar subculture whose ideology has continued to have a profound impact on American society up to the present day. The antiwar movement and corresponding anti-antiwar movement also exposed class tensions within the United States. Ironically, it was the relatively well-to-do young Americans of the student protest movements who were most likely to receive draft deferments from the government. Some went to great lengths to avoid the draft, while those who were drafted could often parlay typing skills or a few business courses into safe assignments, doing administrative tasks away from the front lines. While relatively well-off college students protested the war stateside, young people from lower-class families made up the vast majority of the soldiers who actually fought and died in Vietnam. In this respect, the war was in many ways a working-class war fought by those from poorer, less-educated backgrounds.

NIXON AND VIETNAMIZATION: 1969–1975

EVENTS

1969	Nixon announces policy of Vietnamization and Nixon Doctrine
	Ho Chi Minh dies
1970	United States bombs Viet Cong sites in Cambodia
	Student protests in United States turn violent
1971	Nixon sends forces into Laos
	My Lai court-martial begins
	New York Times publishes Pentagon Papers
1972	Kissinger begins secret negotiations with North Vietnam
	Nixon visits China, USSR
	Last U.S. combat troops leave Vietnam
	Nixon wins reelection
	Nixon authorizes Christmas Bombing in North Vietnam
1973	Cease-fire declared in Vietnam; Last U.S. military personnel leave
	Watergate scandal escalates
	Congress passes War Powers Resolution
1974	Nixon resigns; Ford becomes president
1975	Saigon falls to North Vietnamese

KEY PEOPLE

Richard M. Nixon	37th U.S. president; despite policy of Vietnamization and troop withdrawals, expanded scope of war into Cambodia and Laos; forced peace settlement out of North Vietnam in 1973; resigned amid Watergate scandal in 1974
Henry A. Kissinger	Nixon's national security advisor and later secretary of state; negotiated cease-fire with Le Duc Tho
Le Duc Tho	North Vietnamese emissary who negotiated cease-fire with Kissinger at secret talks in Paris

SUMMARY & ANALYSIS

VIETNAMIZATION AND THE NIXON DOCTRINE

When President **Richard M. Nixon** took office in January 1969, he chose former political science professor **Henry A. Kissinger** as his national security advisor. Kissinger saw Vietnam as a mistake and pushed for disengagement. Not long into his term, Nixon announced a new policy of **Vietnamization** to gradually withdraw the more than 500,000 American soldiers from Vietnam and return control of the war to the South Vietnamese **ARVN**.

Nixon did not intend to abandon Saigon fully—the United States would still fund, supply, and train the ARVN—but hoped that slow troop withdrawals would appease voters at home and reduce the number of troop casualties in the field. He also announced the **Nixon Doctrine**, in which he proclaimed that the United States would honor its current defense commitments but that it would not commit troops anywhere else.

HO CHI MINH'S DEATH

In September 1969, the North Vietnamese leader **Ho Chi Minh** died. He was replaced by **Le Duan**, who became the new head of the North Vietnamese Communist Party. Although North Vietnam lost a powerful ideological figure in Ho, his death did not weaken the Vietnamese nationalist cause.

IMPACT OF NIXON'S NEW POLICIES

Vietnamization and the Nixon Doctrine did reduce combat casualties but also turned U.S. foreign policy upside down. In declaring that the United States would no longer commit troops to stop Communist revolutions abroad, Nixon effectively revoked Eisenhower's, Kennedy's, and Johnson's policies of using the U.S. military to prevent Communism from spreading. Although his predecessors had sent troops to fight Soviet influence in the farthest corners of the world, Nixon believed that the political cost of more dead U.S. servicemen was simply too great.

CAMBODIA

With Vietnamization under way, Nixon and Kissinger still had a few tricks up their sleeves. While reducing U.S. personnel in Vietnam slightly in 1969, they also sought to defeat the North Vietnamese by destroying their supply lines and base camps in neighboring **Cambodia**. Although Cambodia was officially a neutral nation, the NVA had long used its territory to run weapons and troops, circumventing the U.S. soldiers, bombers, and raiding parties that were operating in Vietnamese territory.

In the spring of 1970, Nixon authorized a series of bombing raids in Cambodia and sent both U.S. and ARVN troops across the border, all without the consent or even awareness of Congress. When the secret Cambodian campaign was revealed in a *New York Times* exposé in May 1970, it sent shock waves through the uninformed Congress and the American public. Renewed public outcry and waves of protests eventually convinced Nixon to rescind the order that summer. Nonetheless, he authorized a similar action in March 1971, secretly sending ARVN forces across the border into **Laos**.

GROWING COST

By 1970, the Vietnam conflagration had become the longest war in U.S. history. Nearly 50,000 had already been killed and up to 200,000 wounded. Even though this number paled in comparison to the 100,000 South Vietnamese and more than 500,000 North Vietnamese who had died, many Americans thought the number far too high for the mere defense of a strip of jungle on the other side of the world. Morale had fallen to an all-time low both for the families at home and for the men in the field. Veterans' protest groups such as the **Vietnam Veterans Against the War** became increasingly vocal, attacking U.S. policy after they came home. Because the draft continued to exempt college students and skilled workers, critics increasingly denounced the conflict as a rich man's war but a poor man's fight. Blacks in particular suffered some of the highest casualty rates.

ANGER AT THE MILITARY

In 1971, the U.S. Army court-martialed Lieutenant **William Calley** for his role in the My Lai Massacre of 1968, sentencing him to a life term in prison (although he was later paroled). In a series of congressional hearings that same year, a number of U.S. soldiers confessed either anonymously or publicly that dozens of similar **war crimes** had taken place over the course of the war and claimed that the U.S. military had tacitly supported them.

The court-martial and the hearings turned American public opinion against the U.S. military. For perhaps the first time in U.S. history, antiwar protesters focused their anger not only on the politicians who began and oversaw the war but on the troops in the field as well. Some Americans denounced men in uniform as "baby killers." During a notorious trip to North Vietnam in 1972, prominent American actress **Jane Fonda** made public statements sympathizing with the North Vietnamese government, denouncing U.S. military actions, and condemning U.S. soldiers as "war criminals." The infamous incident earned Fonda the derisive nickname "Hanoi Jane" and incensed many Americans, even those who opposed the war.

THE PENTAGON PAPERS

The U.S. government came under further fire in June 1971 when the *New York Times* published a series of articles about the contents of a secret study that Secretary of Defense Robert S. McNamara had commissioned in 1968. The leaked documents, collectively called the **Pentagon Papers**, detailed U.S. government and military activity in Vietnam since the 1940s. The papers revealed that the U.S. Army, as well as presidents Truman, Eisenhower, Kennedy, and Johnson, had authorized a number of covert actions that increased U.S. involvement in Vietnam unbeknownst to the American public.

The Nixon administration attempted to halt the *Times* series, but a landmark U.S. Supreme Court decision allowed the articles to be published. The Pentagon Papers caused an uproar in the United States and pushed the already unpopular war into even murkier moral territory. Public distrust of the government grew deeper.

Congress's Response

Outraged by the unauthorized invasion of Cambodia and by the double scandal from the My Lai Massacre and the Pentagon Papers, many in Congress took steps to exert more control over the war and to appease the equally angry public. The Senate voted to repeal the Gulf of Tonkin Resolution to reduce the military's unchecked spending power (although the House of Representatives did not follow suit). Congress also reduced the number of years drafted soldiers needed to serve in the army. Finally, the **Twenty-Sixth Amendment** was ratified in 1971 to lower the U.S. voting age from twenty-one to eighteen, on the grounds that the young men serving in Vietnam should have a say in which politicians were running the war.

Negotiations with North Vietnam

By 1972, Nixon had reduced the number of U.S. troops in Vietnam to 150,000. Kissinger, meanwhile, began to negotiate with senior Viet Cong official **Le Duc Tho** at secret meetings in Paris. As these talks progressed, Tho became increasingly stubborn and refused to negotiate, forcing Nixon and Kissinger again to change their strategy. They decided to try to improve relations with Communist China—which was not on good terms with the Soviet Union—to use as a bargaining chip to intimidate both the USSR and North Vietnam.

Nixon and Kissinger thus began secret talks with China. This warming of relations culminated with Nixon's high-profile visit to China in February and March 1972. As expected, the Soviet Union, concerned with the improved U.S.-China relations, moved to bargain as well. Nixon therefore visited the USSR in May 1972—another landmark visit.

U.S. Departure and Nixon's Reelection

Nixon's trip to China succeeded in giving him an advantage in negotiations with North Vietnam. When the NVA crossed the demilitarized zone and invaded South Vietnam in March 1972, Nixon unabashedly authorized an intense bombing campaign of **Hanoi** without fear of repercussion from Moscow or Beijing. On August 23, 1972, the last American ground combat troops departed Vietnam, leaving behind only a small number of military advisors (the last of whom left in March 1973). As the presidential elections of 1972 approached, Nixon clearly had the upper hand: he had warmed relations with China and the USSR, reduced the number of U.S. troops in Vietnam from 500,000 to 30,000, and halted a major NVA advance. He defeated antiwar Democrat **George McGovern** in a landslide.

CHRISTMAS BOMBING AND CEASE-FIRE

When Kissinger's negotiations continued to be hindered by North Vietnamese obstinacy, Nixon became frustrated and authorized the **Christmas Bombing**, an intense bombing campaign of North Vietnam to pressure the country to end the war in late December 1972. The pressure worked, and Kissinger and North Vietnamese officials finally announced a **cease-fire** in January 1973.

Under the terms of the agreement, Nixon pledged to **withdraw** all remaining military personnel from Vietnam and allow the tens of thousands of NVA troops in South Vietnam to remain there, despite the fact that they controlled a quarter of South Vietnamese territory. However, Nixon promised to intervene if North Vietnam moved against the South. In exchange, North Vietnam promised that **elections** would be held to determine the fate of the entire country. Although Nixon insisted that the agreement brought "peace with honor," South Vietnamese leaders complained that the terms amounted to little more than a surrender for South Vietnam.

THE WAR POWERS RESOLUTION

In July 1973, Congress and the American public learned the full extent of the secret U.S. military campaigns in Cambodia. Testimony in congressional hearings revealed that Nixon and the military had been secretly bombing Cambodia heavily since 1969, even though the president and Joint Chiefs of Staff had repeatedly denied the charge. When the news broke, Nixon switched tactics and began bombing Cambodia openly despite extreme public disproval.

Angry, Congress mustered enough votes to pass the November 1973 **War Powers Resolution** over Nixon's veto. The resolution restricted presidential powers during wartime by requiring the president to notify Congress upon launching any U.S. military action abroad. If Congress did not approve of the action, it would have to conclude within sixty to ninety days. In effect, this act made the president accountable to Congress for his actions abroad. Congress also ended the **draft** in 1973 and stipulated that the military henceforth consist solely of paid volunteers. Both the War Powers Resolution and the conversion to an all-volunteer army helped quiet antiwar protesters.

WATERGATE

Despite Nixon's landslide reelection victory, his days in office were numbered; on top of the uproar over the Cambodia bombings, the **Watergate scandal** had broken in late 1972. In short, Nixon had approved a secret burglary of the Democratic Party headquarters at the Watergate Hotel in Washington, D.C., prior to the election, but the burglars were caught. Evidence surfaced that Nixon had authorized illegal measures to discredit prominent Democratic opponents and other people on his personal "enemies list." Ultimately, when it became clear that Nixon himself had broken the law by covering up the scandal, many in the United States began calling for his impeachment.

NVA ADVANCES AND THE FALL OF SAIGON

As the Watergate scandal began to envelop Nixon, North Vietnamese Communist leader **Le Duan** assumed correctly that the United States would not likely intervene in Vietnam, despite Nixon's earlier promises to the contrary. As a result, North Vietnamese troops began to move into South Vietnam in 1974. Nixon resigned in disgrace in August 1974 and was replaced by Vice President **Gerald R. Ford**.

Any hope Ford might have had to salvage Vietnam evaporated in September 1974, when Congress refused to approve sufficient funding for the South Vietnamese army. By the beginning of 1975, defeat was imminent. North Vietnamese forces launched a massive offensive in the spring of 1975, forcing the South Vietnamese troops to retreat. On April 30, 1975, **Saigon** fell to the North Vietnamese, all of Vietnam was united under Communist rule, and the Vietnam War was over.

ASSESSING NIXON'S ROLE

Ironically, Nixon, who had risen to national prominence as a hardline anti-Communist in the 1950s, was the president responsible for U.S. withdrawal from Vietnam, the most visible theater of the Cold War against Communism. Furthermore, Nixon and Kissinger used the lengthy withdrawal from Vietnam as part of a larger vision of **détente**, or thawing of tensions among the superpowers. It is arguable that

Nixon's slow withdrawal took too long and certain that his expansion of the war into Cambodia and Laos was illegal. Nonetheless, Nixon did keep his promise of removing U.S. troops, and it is impressive that he and Kissinger were able to withdraw the United States thoroughly and relatively quickly from the Vietnam quagmire they had inherited from Johnson.

Although Nixon himself made numerous poor decisions and resigned amid scandal, he kept the Vietnam debacle from having a devastating impact on the United States' position in international relations amid the Cold War. Rather, Nixon simultaneously withdrew from Vietnam and achieved improved relations with China and the USSR, easing tension and likely decreasing the threat of nuclear war.

SUMMARY & ANALYSIS

THE AFTERMATH OF THE WAR

LOSSES

The most immediate effect of the Vietnam War was the staggering death toll. The war killed an estimated 2 million Vietnamese civilians, 1.1 million North Vietnamese troops, 200,000 South Vietnamese troops, and 58,000 U.S. troops. Those wounded in combat numbered tens of thousands more. The massive U.S. bombing of both North and South Vietnam left the country in ruins, and the U.S. Army's use of herbicides such as Agent Orange not only devastated Vietnam's natural environment but also caused widespread health problems that have persisted for decades.

THE SOCIALIST REPUBLIC OF VIETNAM

In July 1976, the new unified Vietnam was officially reunited as the **Socialist Republic of Vietnam (SRV)**, with its capital at **Hanoi**. Saigon was renamed **Ho Chi Minh City**. Even though Vietnam had succeeded in evicting the United States, its military problems were not over. In neighboring **Kampuchea** (as Cambodia was now called), Communist dictator **Pol Pot** and his Khmer Rouge forces began a reign of terror in the hope of creating a pre-industrial utopia, murdering around 2 million people in so-called "killing fields."

In 1978, the SRV invaded Kampuchea to stop the Khmer Rouge. Although Vietnam's invasion of Kampuchea put an end to the killing fields, China was threatened by Vietnam's extension of influence in the region and began a border war with Vietnam. After decades of conflict, Vietnam found itself with the world's fourth-largest army but one of the world's poorest economies. In the late 1980s and early 1990s, it began to turn more toward capitalism and a liberal economy.

VIETNAM AND U.S. SOCIETY

By 1975, Vietnam was off the Gallup Poll list of top issues in the United States. Aside from concern for remaining U.S. **prisoners of war (POWs)** still in Vietnam, Americans became less and less concerned with events within the country. Nonetheless, the war had lasting effects. Combined with the Watergate scandal, it inspired widespread public distrust of the U.S. government and made the military less popular, at least in the short term. The draft has not been used since.

The Vietnam War also has played a large role in American popular culture, especially in **film**. Prominent films such as *Taxi Driver* (1976), *Coming Home* (1978), *The Deer Hunter* (1978), *Apocalypse Now* (1979), *Platoon* (1986), *Full Metal Jacket* (1987), and *Born on the Fourth of July* (1989) dealt with topics ranging from the brutality of the war itself to the difficulty of Vietnam veterans' attempts to readjust to American society and cope with war trauma after returning to the United States.

GEOPOLITICAL EFFECTS

In 1975, it appeared that the Vietnam War was a clear loss for the United States. But while much of Indochina did become Communist, validating the domino theory to an extent, the war left mostly psychological scars in the United States. It did not affect the United States' status as a superpower, and though North Vietnam "won" the war, realizing Ho Chi Minh's lifelong dream, Vietnam's postwar period was filled with more fighting, poverty, and suffering for its people. Today, as capitalism makes inroads in Vietnam, one would hardly suspect that Communists won the war in 1975.

The wars in which the United States had previously been involved, especially World War II, had been winner-take-all wars in which few considerations other than ultimate victory or defeat affected U.S. military policy. The Vietnam War was fundamentally different for the United States, as it was essentially a proxy theater of the larger Cold War with the USSR. Vietnam thus was asymmetrical: whereas North Vietnam's objectives were simple and straightforward, the United States was burdened by a whole host of other issues in its dealings. Ultimately, Vietnam was an entirely new kind of war for the United States, one that still remains morally and historically problematic. Though far smaller and more geographically confined than the great world wars earlier in the century, Vietnam completely changed the way the United States approached military action and helped define the role of the United States within the new world order.

Study Questions & Essay Topics

Always use specific historical examples to support your arguments.

Study Questions

1. *How were the Vietnamese Communist forces so effective in the face of the far wealthier, technologically superior powers of France and the United States?*

Vietnamese resistance to foreign rule was based on a centuries-long history of Vietnam fighting against imperial and colonial overlords. Raised on stories of generations of fighting against imperial China, Vietnamese Communists were willing to make tremendous sacrifices and fight patiently for decades. Moreover, the Vietnamese Communist forces had a particularly able body of leaders. In sharp contrast to the corrupt French- and U.S.-backed leadership in southern Vietnam, northern Vietnam's leaders were sincere and passionate about their nationalism. Ho Chi Minh, who exemplified this skillful, unified leadership, had years of experience in the West and appropriated his learning to use against France and the United States.

Strategically, the decentralized command structure of the Vietnamese Communist forces and the agrarian nature of the North Vietnamese economy made it difficult for U.S. bombing campaigns to find targets that would disable Vietnam's military effort. North Vietnam's pre-industrial status negated the impact of military technology that the United States had developed for use against highly industrialized nations such as Germany in World War II. This strategic hurdle, combined with the fact that the Vietnamese Communists were willing to accept an enormous human cost to win the independence of their homeland, made the U.S. task difficult. Battling for vague Cold War principles and unwilling to make such sacrifices, the United States ultimately lacked the will to prevail in the war.

2.   *How did the Tet Offensive affect American politics,*
     society, and the course of the war in Vietnam?

Although the Tet Offensive was one of the greatest tactical victories for the U.S. forces against Viet Cong guerrillas, it was an enormous political loss for the United States during the war. Because the attack intensified the antiwar protest movement at home and discredited President Lyndon Johnson and U.S. military officials, the Tet Offensive represented a major turning point in the war against the United States.

During the Vietnamese New Year, Tet, in January 1968, thousands of Viet Cong insurgents launched the war's largest coordinated attack yet, on nearly thirty U.S. military installations in South Vietnam, along with dozens of other South Vietnamese cities. Although U.S. forces were initially caught off guard, they defeated the guerrillas relatively quickly and decisively—a resounding defeat that permanently crippled Ho Chi Minh's military forces.

Despite this victory, however, the offensive frightened the American public because it seemed to contradict President Johnson's assurances that the United States was winning the war. U.S. public opinion worsened when General William Westmoreland requested 200,000 additional U.S. troops after the offensive, on top of the nearly 500,000 Americans already serving in Vietnam. Westmoreland's request startled not only the American public but also congressmen, senators, foreign-policy makers, and even Johnson himself. Many U.S. government officials privately began to question whether Vietnam was actually "winnable" at all and, if so, whether the United States was using the right tactics. Former secretary of state Dean Acheson voiced his disproval, as did Johnson's own secretary of defense, Robert McNamara, who resigned his position.

The American media compounded the situation, as the official government line that the United States was winning the war contrasted sharply with the shocking images Americans saw on their televisions during the evening news. Westmoreland's request merely confirmed their suspicions that the government was not telling the truth. As a result, more and more Americans began to distrust the federal government and the military. This so-called "credibility gap" between what the government was saying and what was actually happening fueled antiwar activism in the late

1960s and early 1970s. The credibility gap crippled the Democratic Party and effectively ruined Johnson's chances for reelection. Although technically a major military victory, the Tet Offensive was thus a major political defeat for Johnson and the U.S. military and a significant turning point in the war.

3. *Discuss the role the American media played in the Vietnam War.*

During the Vietnam War, the American media did not act simply as a collaborator with the U.S. government as it had in many previous wars; conversely, it served as a powerful check on government power. This dynamic first emerged in January 1963, when journalists reported the defeat of the South Vietnamese army at the Battle of Ap Bac, contrasting sharply with official U.S. government and military reports that the battle had been a victory.

When this power of the media became apparent, some Vietnamese civilians were able to manipulate it, as in June 1963, when a Buddhist monk protesting the U.S.-backed South Vietnamese government burned himself to death in full view of news photographers in the city of Hue. The pictures of the monk's self-immolation appeared on front pages of newspapers across the world and alerted the American public to the corruption of the U.S.-supported Diem regime.

Media resistance to the U.S. government's official statements only increased as the war progressed. The Tet Offensive in 1968, though a tactical victory for the United States, was perceived as a major defeat as the media recast the meaning of the battles. During the Tet offensive, prominent journalist Walter Cronkite editorialized during a nationally televised newscast that it did not look like America could win the war. In 1971, when the *New York Times* and other newspapers published excerpts of the top-secret Pentagon Papers, public distrust of the U.S. government deepened, causing a scandal in the Nixon administration. In the end, this public discontentment had concrete effects, as the antiwar movement became a prominent force and compelled Nixon to start withdrawing U.S. troops. In this sense, Vietnam was very much a "media war," fought in newspapers and on television as much as in the jungles of Vietnam.

SUGGESTED ESSAY TOPICS

1. Did the United States win or lose the Vietnam War? Justify your answer.

2. How did U.S. objectives differ from the objectives of Ho Chi Minh and the Vietnamese Communists during the war?

3. Compare and contrast Johnson's and Nixon's respective Vietnam War strategies.

4. Discuss the impact of antiwar protest movements in the United States during the Vietnam War.

5. How did U.S. foreign policy evolve from the end of World War II in 1945 to the end of the Vietnam War in 1975?

Review & Resources

Quiz

1. Vietnam spent more than a millennium under the imperial rule of

    A. China
    B. India
    C. Japan
    D. Thailand

2. Which of the following was *not* a province of colonial French Indochina?

    A. Annam
    B. Cochin China
    C. Macau
    D. Tonkin

3. All of the following countries ruled Vietnam as an imperial or colonial power at some point *except*

    A. China
    B. Japan
    C. France
    D. Britain

4. Which of the following was the site of a major French defeat in 1954?

    A. Da Nang
    B. Saigon
    C. Dien Bien Phu
    D. My Lai

5. The French established their colonial capital of Vietnam at

    A. Saigon
    B. Hanoi
    C. Hue
    D. Phnom Penh

6. Who was the former emperor of Vietnam whom the French reinstalled as a figurehead in 1949?

    A. Angkor Wat
    B. Bao Dai
    C. My Lai
    D. Pol Pot

7. Who was the U.S.-backed leader of South Vietnam until 1963?

    A. Ho Chi Minh
    B. Le Duc Tho
    C. Ngo Dinh Diem
    D. Vo Nguyen Giap

8. Which international agreement split North Vietnam and South Vietnam in 1954?

    A. The Hanoi Treaty
    B. The Treaty of Versailles
    C. The Geneva Accords
    D. The Helsinki Accords

9. The dividing line between North Vietnam and South Vietnam lay along the

    A. 17th parallel
    B. 23rd parallel
    C. 38th parallel
    D. 42nd parallel

10. What did the domino theory state?

    A. If one country fell to Communism, others nearby would soon follow

    B. Use of nuclear weapons in one country would lead to use in others

    C. If the economy of one Asian country fell, others nearby would soon follow

    D. The United States should increase defense spending to cripple the Soviet economy

11. On which religious group did the Diem regime crack down severely?

    A. Anglicans

    B. Buddhists

    C. Catholics

    D. Hindus

12. In which body of water were two U.S. destroyers allegedly attacked by North Vietnamese forces in August 1964?

    A. The Mekong River

    B. The South China Sea

    C. The Gulf of Thailand

    D. The Gulf of Tonkin

13. Ho Chi Minh was associated with

    A. Communism

    B. Nationalism

    C. Both A and B

    D. Neither A nor B

14. The South Vietnamese "first lady" who was infamous for controversial comments was called

    A. Madame Nhu

    B. Madame Minh

    C. Madame Diem

    D. Madame Butterfly

15. Nixon's secret bombing of Cambodia prompted Congress to pass the

 A. Gulf of Tonkin Resolution
 B. War Powers Resolution
 C. Elkins Act
 D. Teller Amendment

16. In 1963, a Buddhist monk protesting Diem's regime killed himself in public by

 A. Jumping off a cliff
 B. Setting himself on fire
 C. Refusing to move out of the way of an ARVN tank
 D. Drinking poison

17. Which of the following men was *not* assassinated?

 A. Ngo Dinh Diem
 B. John F. Kennedy
 C. Robert F. Kennedy
 D. Lyndon B. Johnson

18. The policy of Vietnamization called for

 A. Bombing North Vietnam around the clock to convince it to surrender
 B. Escalating the war and putting as many troops in South Vietnam as possible
 C. Reducing the number of American troops in South Vietnam and turning control of the war over to the South Vietnamese
 D. Bombing Laos and Cambodia in order to destroy NVA supply lines

19. What did COINTELPRO do?

    A. Hunted for Soviet spies in Washington, D.C.
    B. Hunted for NVA spies near U.S. bases in South Vietnam
    C. Investigated war crimes allegations against U.S. military officials
    D. Harassed and arrested antiwar protesters in the United States

20. The Viet Cong raid at Pleiku gave Johnson justification to begin

    A. Vietnamization
    B. Operation Rolling Thunder
    C. The Tet Offensive
    D. The Christmas Bombing

21. What did the 1964 Gulf of Tonkin Resolution do?

    A. Gave the president more freedom to conduct military operations in Vietnam
    B. Gave the president almost unlimited funding to wage war
    C. Effectively declared war on North Vietnam
    D. All of the above

22. Why did many South Vietnamese resent U.S. military participation in the Vietnam War?

    A. They hated the United States' puppet governments in Saigon
    B. The United States inflicted serious damage to the landscape and on the population
    C. They viewed the war as more of a civil war than an international conflict
    D. All of the above

REVIEW & RESOURCES

23. After the 1968 Tet Offensive, General Westmoreland

    A.   Pressured U.S. policy makers to end the war
    B.   Pressured the British and the Australians to enter the war
    C.   Asked Congress for more U.S. troops
    D.   Pushed for Vietnamization

24. Which of the following did *not* contribute to U.S. paranoia about Communism in the late 1940s?

    A.   The Cuban Missile Crisis
    B.   The Berlin blockade
    C.   Mao Zedong's takeover in China
    D.   The first Soviet atomic bomb test

25. The Viet Cong proved a formidable enemy for all of the following reasons *except*

    A.   Its members believed passionately in the Vietnamese nationalist cause
    B.   Its members could disappear easily into the Vietnamese peasant population
    C.   Its firepower was superior to U.S. firepower
    D.   It had constructed a vast network of underground tunnels and hideouts

26. Which of the following played an unforeseen, important role in the Vietnam War?

    A.   The Soviet Red Army
    B.   Cuban guerrilla fighters
    C.   The American media
    D.   The Roman Catholic Church

27. All of the following were associated with the U.S. antiwar movement *except*

    A.   Barry M. Goldwater
    B.   "Teach-ins"
    C.   The counterculture
    D.   J. William Fulbright

28. Why did Nixon initiate warmer relations with China in 1972?

   A.   Because he worried that nuclear war was imminent
   B.   To gain leverage in Vietnam
   C.   To gain leverage against Japan
   D.   Because he had a penchant for Chinese culture

29. The Nixon Doctrine stipulated that

   A.   The United States must do everything in its power to fight Soviet aggression
   B.   The United States would no longer send troops abroad to fight Communism
   C.   The United States must assist in global development efforts
   D.   The United States must escalate the war in Vietnam in accordance with the domino theory

30. What is napalm?

   A.   A type of plastic explosive
   B.   A poison applied to the tips of bullets
   C.   A flammable gasoline-based gel
   D.   A chemical herbicide and defoliant

31. All of the following statements about the Pentagon Papers are true *except*

   A.   They were originally commissioned by Robert McNamara
   B.   They surfaced after being leaked to a Viet Cong spy
   C.   The White House attempted to block their publication
   D.   They angered the American public

32. Which U.S. official tried to negotiate an end to the war through secret talks with Viet Cong official Le Duc Tho?

   A.   Henry A. Kissinger
   B.   McGeorge Bundy
   C.   J. William Fulbright
   D.   Robert S. McNamara

REVIEW & RESOURCES

33. With which president is the policy of Vietnamization associated?

    A.   Eisenhower
    B.   Kennedy
    C.   Johnson
    D.   Nixon

34. With which president is the policy of Americanization associated?

    A.   Eisenhower
    B.   Kennedy
    C.   Johnson
    D.   Nixon

35. The failed U.S. initiative to relocate Vietnamese peasants to specific villages was called the

    A.   "Hearts and minds" program
    B.   "Hanoi Hilton" program
    C.   "Strategic enclave" program
    D.   "Strategic hamlet" program

36. The My Lai Massacre of 1968 turned American public opinion against

    A.   The South Vietnamese
    B.   The North Vietnamese
    C.   Nixon
    D.   The U.S. military

37. The Viet Cong differed from the NVA in that

    A.   The United States fought the NVA but not the Viet Cong
    B.   The NVA were professional soldiers, whereas the Viet Cong were civilian guerrillas
    C.   The United States fought the Viet Cong but not the NVA
    D.   There was no difference; they were the same organization

38. Hubert Humphrey lost the presidential election of 1968 partly because of his association with

    A.   The Chicago Riot
    B.   The Pentagon Papers
    C.   The My Lai Massacre
    D.   Woodstock

39. Johnson and the military's request for more troops in 1968 coupled with their assurances that the United States was winning the war in Vietnam helped form the

    A.   "Crisis of confidence"
    B.   "Johnson Doctrine"
    C.   "Credibility gap"
    D.   "Reality check"

40. Which of the following did *not* cause a scandal in the Nixon administration?

    A.   The Cambodia bombings
    B.   The Pentagon Papers
    C.   Nixon's visit to China
    D.   The Watergate break-in

41. On which president's watch did the largest increases in U.S. troop numbers in Vietnam occur?

    A.   Eisenhower
    B.   Kennedy
    C.   Johnson
    D.   Nixon

42. Nixon used the term "silent majority" to refer to Americans who supported

    A.   U.S. action in Vietnam
    B.   His resignation
    C.   Student protesters
    D.   The North Vietnamese

43. Which Constitutional amendment lowered the U.S. voting age from twenty-one to eighteen?

   A.   The Twenty-Fourth Amendment
   B.   The Twenty-Fifth Amendment
   C.   The Twenty-Sixth Amendment
   D.   The Twenty-Seventh Amendment

44. All of the following eroded the American public's support for the war *except*

   A.   The Tet Offensive
   B.   The My Lai Massacre
   C.   The Pentagon Papers
   D.   The Nixon Doctrine

45. What was the COSVN?

   A.   A war planning committee created by the Joint Chiefs of Staff
   B.   The South Vietnamese army
   C.   A branch of the FBI that targeted U.S. antiwar protesters
   D.   A Viet Cong command center that may or may not have existed

46. Which famous actress made a notorious 1972 visit to North Vietnam?

   A.   Glenn Close
   B.   Jane Fonda
   C.   Meryl Streep
   D.   Sigourney Weaver

47. Sporadic incidents in which U.S. soldiers killed their own superior officers in order not to be sent on combat missions were referred to as

   A.   "Flagging"
   B.   "Flogging"
   C.   "Fragging"
   D.   "Frogging"

48. Saigon finally fell to North Vietnamese forces in

    A. 1971
    B. 1973
    C. 1975
    D. 1977

49. What was Vietnam officially called beginning in 1976?

    A. The Democratic Republic of Vietnam
    B. The Republic of Vietnam
    C. The Socialist Republic of Vietnam
    D. The United States of Vietnam

50. Who succeeded Ho Chi Minh as head of the Vietnamese
    Communist Party upon Ho's death?

    A. Le Duan
    B. Le Duc Tho
    C. Ngo Dinh Diem
    D. Pol Pot

SUGGESTIONS FOR FURTHER READING

CAPUTO, PHILIP. *A Rumor of War*. New York: Owl Books, 1996.

HALBERSTAM, DAVID. *The Best and the Brightest*. New York: Fawcett, 1993.

HERR, MICHAEL. *Dispatches*. New York: Vintage, 1991.

KARNOW, STANLEY. *Vietnam: A History*. New York: Penguin, 1997.

KENNEDY, DAVID M., LIZABETH COHEN, AND THOMAS A. BAILEY. *The American Pageant*. Boston: Houghton Mifflin, 2002.

O'BRIEN, TIM. *The Things They Carried*. New York: Broadway, 1998.

SPECTOR, RONALD H. *After Tet: The Bloodiest Year in Vietnam*. New York: Vintage, 1994.

SUMMERS, ANTHONY. *The Arrogance of Power: The Secret World of Richard Nixon*. New York: Penguin, 2000.

YOUNG, MARILYN B. *The Vietnam Wars: 1945–1990*. New York: HarperCollins, 1991.

.

Try our SparkCharts (only $4.95):

Easy-to-read, laminated chart that fits directly into your notebook or binder.

Also Available:

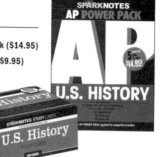